REVISED EDITION

DOWNLINE LEADERSHIP

BLUEPRINT FOR NETWORK MARKETING LEADERS

A 10 week intensive leadership development program

ERIC WALTON

Downline Leadership blew my mind. Eric has a way of pulling out the good things in people, making them think, and challenging them to challenge themselves in a practical way. Building a business and leading a team takes so much more than numbers and sales pitches, and the skills Eric teaches are the missing piece. As I excitedly posted in our group about halfway through this class, "I'm not stuck anymore!"

—Carolyn Young, Young Living Gold leader

If you are looking for a way to support your members in an impactful way that will also help them grow individually as leaders and together as a team, the *Downline Leadership* training is it! I went through the program with five leaders and am amazed at the new unity, friendships, and skills we all gained. The material is geared specifically to our business, with examples that we can all relate to. This has been so powerful that I'm now using this material and group style with my team! Builders are shifting their thinking, owning their businesses, and creating amazing momentum! Highly recommend this program and Eric's facilitation!

—Britta Dimler, Young Living Diamond leader

I joined in on this course thinking that I would learn a series of do's and don'ts on what it takes to be a good leader, much like what I've learned from the other books that I have read on leadership. Instead, I learned foundational principles that I was given the opportunity to practice and adopt into my own leadership style. This course ended up changing me and my definition of what a leader is. Eric Walton is the very definition of a leader, and I can't think of a better person to learn these valuable principles from. If you are a leader of any kind—mother, father, boss, entrepreneur, etc.—I highly encourage you to read this book and take this course if you are able.

—Paula Garcia, Young Living Gold leader

I've invested in a lot of leadership development and training over the years, but NOTHING has been more transformational than the lessons in *Downline Leadership*. My team members have noticed the difference, and a huge weight has been lifted off of me as I've learned to transition from a burned-out director to a mentor and, better yet, a coach. If you want to eliminate say-do gaps, create a culture of co-ownership, build trust and influence as a leader, and find YOUR "one road to diamond," this book is for you.

—Kristin Warnaca, Young Living Gold leader

Eric's *Downline Leadership* was exactly what I needed and one of the best investments I've ever made. It was a catalyst both for launching my business successfully and, surprisingly, for some major personal growth that has powerfully and positively impacted every relationship I have! I highly recommend this if you are ready to take your professional and personal growth to the next level! Eric's attention to detail and his authenticity and transparency are rare, and I am so grateful to have had this opportunity.

—Amy De Bois, Young Living Silver leader

Eric helped me prioritize key areas in which to be a highly effective leader while at the same time providing the tools needed to complete daily tasks that are specific for my team. He helped me fill in the missing pieces, which I had been searching for, and I was able to quickly apply those pieces to my team with immediate success. Eric was able to help me overcome fears I didn't even know I had, which heightened my purpose with Young Living. I now know what my road to Diamond looks like and how to get there! *Downline Leadership* is a powerful tool for new or seasoned leaders. I will be using this as a tool with my team for years to come.

—Carolyn Russell, Young Living Silver leader

I cannot speak highly enough about the *Downline Leadership* program and Eric's facilitation of it. I decided to participate since I had no previous business or leadership experience. I was hoping to learn practical skills and gain confidence. I not only left with my expectations met, but with them far exceeded as I learned further about how to harness my strengths as a connector while having tangible action items to address the areas that require more attention in my downline. I highly recommend this book and program! There is something for everyone.

—Rosy Crescitelli, Young Living Platinum Leader

Downline Leadership is a book that every serious Young Living leader needs to get into their hands today! It has truly transformed me as a person and leader. As a result of incorporating these principles, I have seen tremendous growth in my YL organization! The leadership skills Eric shares are truly invaluable! This is a book that will take you to the next level in the short term, and its principles are vital for you to continue growing to Diamond and beyond! It's the best investment Young Living leaders can make for the development and growth of their team! I know I will refer to it again and again as our team navigates growth related challenges! Highly recommended!

—Stephanie Long, Young Living Silver leader

Eric Walton's *Downline Leadership* program is a critical component for a growing leader wanting to rock their business! This book helps to establish vision, confidence, relationships, and pertinent leadership skills for every leader no matter their rank!

—Garen Garza, Young Living Senior Star leader

Downline Leadership
Blueprint for Network Marketing Leaders
A 10 week intensive leadership development program
By Eric Walton

Copyright © 2018 Building Up Leaders, LLC
Published by SkillBites Publishing

ISBN-10:1-942489-69-2
ISBN-13:978-1-942489-69-6

TABLE OF CONTENTS

Dedication..vii

Acknowledgments vii

Introduction 1

MODULE 1: Downline Leadership..7

MODULE 2: Leadership Engine 21

MODULE 3: Communication 43

MODULE 4: Coaching 63

MODULE 5: Ownership and Accountability 83

MODULE 6: Intuition 105

MODULE 7: Overcoming Challenges 121

MODULE 8: Innovation...139

MODULE 9: Balance and Agility 155

MODULE 10: Leaving a Legacy 167

Eric Walton 182

DEDICATION

This book is dedicated to my wife, Tammy. Way before she became a Diamond with Young Living, she was my diamond for life. Tammy, thank you so much for your never-ending patience and support for this book. If it weren't for your love, encouragement, and insight, I would certainly not have written it. You are the most amazing leader I know, and your downline reflects that!

ACKNOWLEDGMENTS

Thank you to:

Julie Gutierrez, who has been my editor, co-coach, and friend. Thank you for always believing in this story and me.

Andrea Johanson, who helped me as an editor, and more importantly, saw things from the perspective of the everyday mom and distributor.

Janell Vonigas, for her work on the cover art with a little help from Sarah Newquist.

Suzi Hersey, who proofread every page and found things no one else could have.

Kristin Warnaca, who was responsible for bringing the revised edition to life.

Sarah, Kristin, Andrea, Julie, Tammy, Vida, Pam, Trish, and Stacy, who sat through this program for the first time and helped me rewrite, rewrite, and rewrite.

Judy Weintraub and the incredible publishing team at SkillBites for your hard work getting the words on the screen to show up in print.

INTRODUCTION

Welcome to Downline Leadership, the blueprint for network marketing leaders. This book is specifically designed to help you improve your leadership in this crazy and wonderful multi-level marketing (MLM) world. While the book is applicable to almost every MLM business, the stories in most modules are written from my wife's and my experience in achieving the Diamond Rank with Young Living essential oils.

Each of the ten modules has been carefully crafted to strengthen your leadership while pulling the very best from you. We highly recommend that you engage with this material in a programmed fashion by participating in a small group led by a Certified Downline Leadership coach/facilitator. You can find our certified coaches and new group launch dates at www.buildingupleaders.com. This program approach utilizes three components: reading the Downline Leadership Book, active engagement in your small group, and intentional application of your leadership learning. You will find that the reading will challenge your beliefs about leadership. During the group sessions, you will have the chance to share your successes and challenges with other leaders who are on the same journey as you. During the week's in-between sessions, you will have the opportunity to apply what you are learning. Please note that if you do not engage in a Downline Leadership group, that's OK, you can still utilize this book in a systemic fashion to grow your leadership. Just answer the questions at the end of each module and apply what you've learned during the week, then go on to the next module. Why do all this? Because...

> "Everything rises and falls on leadership."
>
> –John Maxwell
>
> The 21 Indispensable Qualities of a Leader. John Maxwell (p. XI). 1999, Nashville, TN by Thomas Nelson

This wonderful quote from John Maxwell applies to each of our distributorship businesses. The question becomes: How do we increase our leadership?

The Downline Leadership book and program is designed to answer that exact question! We will show you how important the ability to develop relationships is to increasing your leadership and what it means to gain influence with your team and downline.

In the end, we all desire to touch more lives and build a thriving business—and we want to help others do the same! In this book and program, you will learn how to use your leadership to achieve those goals and others. Here are three critical questions to answer:

1. Do I want my business to succeed?

2. Do I want to be a leader people follow?

3. Do I want to develop other leaders?

If the answer to each of these questions is "Yes," then you've come to the right place!

The questions and answers are important because it is *your* passion, *your* interest in personal development, and *your* willingness to do the work that will determine how far you progress. As with anything worthwhile, what you put into this program will determine what you get out of it.

This book and program are designed to play a key role in your journey of leadership development. As a business owner, you may have already invested time, effort, and passion toward your growth and development, both personally and professionally. It's also possible you may have applied some of the principles and leadership dimensions we will discuss. Regardless of where you are on this continuum, learning and growing is a lifelong endeavor, and you can be assured this book and program will help further accelerate your ongoing efforts. We will help you gain new leadership insights into yourself and your team, as well as teach you how to incorporate leadership into your business and life.

We will help you take stock of your current leadership inventory, your varied experiences, and your viewpoints. As you work together with your colleagues, a more enhanced approach to leadership will develop through shared knowledge and feedback.

The material in this book and program focuses on helping you to make changes within yourself and your leadership that will leave a positive and lasting leadership legacy. We don't talk about "doing" leadership; we encourage you to determine who you want to be as a leader and then be it.

The format of the program is quite simple. Each week, you will be provided with a new module that describes a particular leadership competency. During the week prior to your group session, you are asked to read the material and answer the questions in the four quadrants found on the last page of the module. The material is foundational in nature and reviews timeless leadership lessons.

At the group session, we don't reteach the material. Instead, we talk about how you would apply the lesson to yourself. The magic happens in the group session. Your coach facilitates the session, ensures everyone is engaged and has equal air time, and asks lots of open-ended questions seeking your insight and leadership perspective. Near the end of the session, we have a Story, where one of the participants in the group plays the role of Storyteller and shares with us a challenge he or she is going through. The rest of the group then asks open-ended questions to help the Storyteller solve his or her own problem. We end the meeting by asking for a leadership-related action item from each participant that each commit to do during the week. We follow up at the next session by asking how it went for each person. The secret to the program is *applying* these lessons to your business and team.

There are foundational themes that permeate this book and coaching program, and it would be good to introduce you to them so you will recognize them while going through the different competencies.

- Self-awareness—Your understanding of who you are impacts everything you think or do, and the level of your self-awareness directly affects your future as a leader. We will encourage you to look inward frequently to help you stay grounded as you grow your leadership.

- Legacy—Everything you do and say leaves a legacy with those around you. During this program you will focus on leaving a positive leadership legacy as you work on improving your leadership skills.

- Ownership—Leaders own it! During this program, not only do we encourage you to own everything about your business, we will introduce the concept of co-ownership to you. You will learn to look at your downline not as employees, but as partners and co-owners in your journey. We all own it together.

- Emotional Intelligence—Managers focus on IQ, being reactive, and handling the tasks at hand. Leaders focus on EQ (emotional intelligence), being proactive with their relationships, their team, and how they are affecting and influencing people.

- Replication vs. Duplication—Your job is not to copy or duplicate yourself. Your responsibility is to replicate yourself in other leaders by modeling leadership. Show them your very best and challenge them to find the best in themselves. Good leaders develop themselves; great leaders develop others. In this program, we encourage you to do both! Remember, replicate your leadership and duplicate your systems.

- Situational Leadership—Leaders are agile and quick to change their approach, style, and role when the situation requires it. Leaders use their intuition, combined with open-ended coaching questions, to know which role to adapt to in order to be the most effective leader they can be.

Let's close this introduction by sharing with you the different leadership competencies we will be going through.

Downline Leadership Program Competencies

Module	Definition	Behaviors of Leaders, They:
Downline Leadership	*The act of connecting, engaging, and influencing your team and downline toward success.*	• Focus on leading people, not just managing the process. • See themselves as the leader of their business, their team, and their downline. • Understand that true success is achieved when they replicate themselves and their leadership in others.
Leadership Engine	*Establishing credibility, developing relationships, earning trust, and gaining influence with your team and downline.*	• Are vulnerable, present, and competent to establish credibility. • Extend themselves outward to connect with their downlines. • Genuinely care about the people on their teams and downlines. • Trust others first, having faith in their teams. • Focus on eliminating any Say/Do gaps to earn trust. • Work hard to gain influence with others through their relationships and performance.
Communication	*Listening, caring, sharing, and connecting with your team and downline.*	• Listen to the emotions; speak with the team, not at the team. • Exhibit empathy to put themselves in the shoes of their downlines. • Say the right thing, at the right time, to the right person, in the right way.
Coaching	*Being a catalyst for the growth and development of others.*	• Seek to understand first by asking open-ended questions. • Invest time into the growth and development of their teams, helping each to discover their own "WHY." • See the long-term value of people.
Ownership and Accountability	*When you lay claim to something as being completely yours and accept the responsibility that drives leaders and teams toward success.*	• Don't give excuses, or point fingers, or get defeated. Accept plain and simple ownership for everything about their business. • Overcome obstacles and get things done. They own it! • Help their team to take ownership over the team's business, the team's situation, and the team's future. • Hold themselves accountable first. • Emphasize personal accountability and say/do alignment to create an accountability culture.
Intuition	*The ability to combine the hard data of the physical world with the soft data of the emotional world— and make a decision to move forward.*	• Gain insight into, and better understanding of, the other person and his or her issues and concerns. • Know where to invest their time. • Are able to take action quicker and more effectively when using their intuition.

Downline Leadership Program Competencies (cont.)

Module	Definition	Behaviors of Leaders, They:
Overcoming Challenges	Removing the obstacles, ambiguity, and issues that hinder progress.	• Set the tone for the whole team with the right mindset when faced with a challenge. • Will pause, analyze, and assess a challenge before jumping in and attempting to solve it. • Work hard to bring clarity to situations that are filled with ambiguity.
Innovation	The ability to think of creative ideas and put them into action.	• Foster an innovative culture/environment within the team. • Exhibit an innovative attitude and thought process.
Balance and Agility	Finding stability by being flexible and responsive to the needs of the business.	• Strive for balance between competing forces that impact their leadership of the Team. • Utilize situational leadership and agility when choosing the leadership style they will deploy.
Leaving a Legacy	The lasting contribution and impact you leave with others	• Invest into others, their relationships, their coaching, and their development. • Develop other leaders.

Let's move on to our first competency!

DOWNLINE LEADERSHIP

Leadership….Everyone wants it. Everyone needs it. However, few know what it is and even fewer know how to get it. In this book and program, we're going to help you better understand what Downline Leadership is, how to develop yours, and most importantly, how to develop it in others.

> *"If your actions inspire others to dream more, learn more, do more and become more, you are a leader."*
>
> –John Quincy Adams

We see Downline Leadership as a full circle of influence. Effective Downline Leaders know how to lead their upline, their downline, crossline, and themselves. **Leadership begins and ends with you, and it's ALWAYS about them.** Interesting paradox, right? Keep this me/them perspective in mind as you go through this module and program. Leadership is all about who *you* are, but it gets measured in how *they* are impacted. NOTE: "They" and "Them" are the people on your team.

Module Overview

As a result of finishing this module, you will

- Discover your unique strengths and weaknesses as a leader and what it means to see yourself as one.

- See the opportunity to become the leader of your team and influencer of your downline and upline.

- Accelerate the integration of your management and leadership skill sets.

- Be introduced to the Downline Success Formula.

- Explore what it means to be *that* leader—the one everyone follows and the one who has a great amount of influence throughout his or her team and downline.

What is Downline Leadership?

Downline Leadership is the act of connecting, engaging, and influencing your team and downline toward success. Let's break this down into its component definitions. Downline is all of the people in your organization, including businesspeople and customers. Team means the fellow leaders who are on this network marketing journey with you. The ones that are all in! Success is defined by each person and is generally in the direction of fulfillment, satisfaction, and goals achieved.

We're going to use the words above (along with some others) often in the book, so let's spend a little bit more time on these definitions, starting with *success*.

Success

Success is incredibly important to leaders. When you're working with your team, it's critical that you define what success means to each of them and to you. Why? Without doing so, there's no direction for you or them.

For some, it will be simple—"enough money to pay for my own product"; for others, it will be more complex, with multiple moving parts, such as "hit the next rank." Many will see success as consistent growth in business, increased number of lives touched and impacted by them, and replication of leaders in their team and downline. Either way, you have to know *their* definition AND this definition has to tie to *their* **why.**

Each person has a why—the reason they're in this business. When you know each person's why and their definition of success, you're ready to begin leading. You can connect to their why by developing stronger relationships. In a later module, we'll discuss the importance of relationships for successful leadership to occur, and it will become even clearer why knowing your team members' definitions of success is critical to you as a leader.

Downline Management

Downline Management can be defined as the tactical discipline of organizing and managing the tasks, resources, schedule, and budget of your business. It includes the enrollment of new businesspeople and customers and the maintenance of your team. Taking care of the day-to-day running of your business while supporting your team and downline is hugely critical work that must be done, or there will be no one to lead. And... your management focus is much different than your leadership focus.

Downline Leadership

Downline Leadership is focused on *leading people* to achieve their definition of success. Downline Leaders help their teammates overcome problems, explore new ways to improve relationships, achieve powerful results, and deliver lasting value to other people.

People

We believe that *the* missing ingredient in many networking marketing businesses is the emphasis on PEOPLE. There's virtually no downline that exists without people being directly involved in some facet. To become an effective leader, you need to continually improve your skill sets in interacting with, influencing, and leading people.

Self-awareness

The first person you must address on your journey to becoming a stronger leader is YOU! That takes commitment, self-awareness, and examination. Throughout this book, you will be challenged to look inward first. Here are a few questions to ask yourself that can also be used to help others:

- How do we realize our potential?

- What is our purpose and goal?

- What open-ended questions have we asked ourselves?

- What role models do we like, and why?

- What stories can we tell about ourselves?

- Where has our success been?

- What do we love to create?

- What situations can we put ourselves in that will showcase our strengths?

Each of the leadership competencies in the Downline Leadership program encourages you to look inward to yourself and outward to your interactions with other members of the team. When you can lead yourself and effectively influence others toward their goals, you've become a leader.

Downline Success

In this book, you will learn how to build credibility, develop relationships, earn trust, and gain influence that impacts people. You will discover how to create a leadership culture that supports accountability, impactful execution, and innovation while helping people with their businesses. You'll learn how to wear different hats, such as Director, Teacher, Mentor, or Coach, and why it's important to leave a valuable leadership legacy. Most importantly, you'll learn the Downline Success Formula and how to implement it in your business:

| Level of DOWNLINE SUCCESS | = | DOWNLINE Management COMPETENCY | ✗ | DOWNLINE Leadership EFFECTIVENESS |

The level of Downline Success achieved is based on your competency as a Downline Manager, multiplied by your effectiveness as a Downline Leader. It's important to note that it is the combination of both your Downline Management and Downline Leadership skills that yields the greatest downline results.

Why "×" and not "+" in the formula? Because Downline Leadership effectiveness is a force multiplier, and when you are at the height of your abilities as a leader, you are able to leverage the combined positive impact of more than just yourself. Through your influence and development of others, you will positively impact people and their downlines toward their definition of success.

Why is Downline Management expertise not enough?

How is it possible that a downline that is well managed fails to achieve its goals? Frequently, it's due to a lack of leadership. The team needs someone to rally them when things are stalled, guide them when the direction gets murky, and coach them when they're stuck. They need someone to influence them in a new direction, celebrate when a milestone is reached, or hold them accountable to achieve goals they have set for themselves. They need a leader!

Story Time!

During the course of this book and program, we'll share stories about leaders and their experiences. Often, you'll see yourself in the story and be able to relate. Time for a story to see what we can learn from it.

Nothing was working, until...

Alesha had been struggling to get her team to respond to her Facebook posts. Her desperation was beginning to show because her posts on her business page were becoming longer, more frequent, and more anxious in nature.

The company she works with does some pretty nice monthly promotions. This month's was particularly good and she really wanted her businesspeople to take full advantage of its value. She knew this could bring some welcomed momentum to her team and to their bottom line, so out of her desire to make something happen, she posted about it every day for a week. She was hoping it would create some excitement and momentum within her team and that they would, in turn, take it to their own teams and customers. But nothing happened. Alesha's frustration was building. She was beside herself because her team wasn't taking advantage of the promotion. NO ONE was. They weren't ordering themselves and they weren't sharing it with their teams or with their customers. This special was over the top and Alesha knew that her team would do well with it if they just shared it.

With her frustration rising to an all-time high, Alesha was about to give up when she got a call from her upline, Lori.

Lori: Hey Alesha, how are you doing?

Alesha: Not too good. Actually, I'm really frustrated. I've been trying to get my businesspeople excited about this month's promotion, and it seems like NO ONE cares. I'm done; I'm not going to post about it anymore, and I'm just going to move on.

Lori: I'm so sorry to hear that Alesha. Why do you think they don't care?

Alesha: Because I've been posting every day on our team page and I'm getting no response. No one has acknowledged my posts.

Lori: Well...how else could you reach out to them?

Alesha: I've always reached out to them this way, it's how I like to communicate.

Lori: What would it look like if you made some phone calls or did a couple of video chats with some key people and asked them what their thoughts are on the promo and how they think it would be best to get it out to their business team and customers? What do you think about trying that?

Alesha: I don't have the time to make calls. I shouldn't have to call each person individually. I'm busy and have too much on my plate. I feel like they should take ownership and responsibility for their own businesses. These promotions are a monthly gift, and I don't understand why they don't take advantage of them.

Lori: I hear your frustration, but I'm just wondering...What do you think your team thinks about your posts? What do you think they think about you?

That stopped Alesha in her tracks. Lori had never challenged her so directly before. How was she to respond? This whole touchy/feely conversation didn't sit well with Alesha at all. But, maybe, just maybe there was something to Lori's questions. Alesha thanked Lori deeply for getting her to pause and simply reflect. Alesha thought to herself, "You know what? I'm going to call Kate and see what she thinks of all of this."

Alesha: Kate, I'm so glad I was able to get ahold of you. Do you have a minute?

Kate: Sure, Alesha, what's up?

Alesha: Have you seen my Facebook posts on this month's promotion?

Kate: Yup! I've seen them—ALL of them.

Alesha: What do you think of them?

Kate: To be honest Alesha, when I read some of your posts I feel like you're talking AT me and not WITH me. The promos seem great, but I don't know how to introduce them to my team. I would really like help on how to share their value. I've never used any of those products before, so I really don't know how to talk about them. And I certainly don't know how to ask someone to spend extra money on something if I don't know how it's going to help the person.

Alesha: Hmm...You've got a really good point. I really need to find a way to talk about the promo more effectively. I just assumed everyone knew what I know. I guess I've been so busy telling everyone about the promos that I forgot to actually create a dialogue with everyone to find out how they feel about the promos and how they would like to share them with their teams and customers. Kate, thanks for talking this out with me. I'm going to take a different approach on my next post and I'll reach out to a few folks to get their buy-in and support, too. I really appreciate the talk. This was so helpful. Can I call you back so we can work on this promo communication together?

Kate: I'm glad I was able to help, Alesha. I'm happy you called me, and I loved talking with you. And YES, I'd really like to work on this with you, together!

Discussion

What happened here? What did you learn about Alesha? Lori?

What kinds of questions were coming from Lori? Closed or open-ended?

What type of leadership was Alesha showing? What do you think of Kate's reaction to the discussion?

What would you do next?

What Does a Downline Leader Look Like?

Downline Leaders are transformational. That means you bring about change in those around you. Leaders are disruptive. They don't like the status quo; they want to find breakthroughs. Leaders drive to bring out the very best in people. Let's paint this picture more fully with a list!

Downline Leaders:

- Motivate—Leaders put the fire under you. They help you to see the light at the end of the tunnel and cause you to want to get there.

- Encourage and praise—Leaders uplift you, not tear you down. They are constantly offering words of hope, and the compliments are always flowing.

- Inspire and challenge—Leaders influence you to be great! They move past just getting the task done to getting that championship ring. They run the hills with you, taking on those same challenges to model what it takes to be great.

- Decide—Leaders move forward by making decisions. Even bad decisions are frequently better than no decision at all. It's easier to change the direction of the team if it's moving than if it's standing still.

- Communicate—Leaders actually try to over-communicate. Does everyone know what's going on? Did they catch the last email from Corporate? Leaders make sure *everyone* gets the message, and they do it effectively.

- Provide and receive feedback—Leaders care about the members of the team, so they make the extra effort to provide feedback, even when it might be difficult to give or receive. AND…they are open to receiving feedback from others!

- Reach out when they need help—Leaders are humble and transparent. They ask for help before it's too late.

- Replicate themselves—They empower others to be leaders by modeling leadership to them.

What examples can you think of where you took the actions above?

Do You See Yourself as a Leader?

In both our research and experience, we've found several reasons why people don't flex their leadership muscles. Some struggle with a victim mentality, some are too dependent on the mechanical aspects of management, and others don't have a true awareness about their leadership skills and believe they're not leaders.

Remember, none of the people on your team and downline work for you. They don't report to you. They all own their own businesses. You can't fire them. You can't order them to take a particular action. What are you to do? **Lead them!** But… how?

Let's review the basic steps involved with the leadership development path you need to be on:

1. **See yourself as a leader.** This is a critical first step; it's an open door to self-awareness. Recognizing that you're a leader is the catalyst for your journey. Once you see yourself as a leader, you close off the doors of victimhood, excuse, and constraints.

2. **Increase your self-awareness.** Self-awareness is the capacity to be introspective and understand how we relate to others. It provides the foundation for growth and development. It allows for each of us to be unique in our strengths and weaknesses and creates the room to grow.

3. **Gain and use influence to lead.** Only through influence can you lead your team. You will need to establish your credibility, build relationships, and earn trust to gain influence. And once you have influence, your leadership will soar!

4. **Create feedback loops.** Feedback loops provide valuable insight into your actions. They happen when you have strong relationships that lead to trust. In a trusting environment, you can continue to build and strengthen your leadership with the help of others through the feedback they give you.

   Here's a quick summary of what a feedback loop looks like:

   a. Determine what you want feedback on.

   b. Talk with someone whom you trust to provide the feedback. Be specific in your request. Do this BEFORE your action.

    c. Take an action.

    d. The action has one or more effects.

    e. Observations and feedback on your action (and results) are presented back to you by the person you had talked to earlier.

    f. This loop is repeated regularly.

To assist you with seeing yourself as a leader, we'll share concepts to stimulate your thinking. Reviewing these concepts will help you decide how to approach the content of this book and what to get out of it:

- Leader as Owner

- Leading By Example

- Integrating Downline Management with Downline Leadership

Leader as Owner

We will discuss "Ownership" in a later module, but let's briefly touch on it now. It helps you to better see yourself as a leader when you see yourself as the OWNER of your business. Our view is that leaders are the complete owners of their businesses. They own what happens in their business. You may be thinking, "That's crazy! My downline comprises independent distributors and I don't have the type of power that can change everything they do!"

BUT, you do! Leadership is what changes culture, and that leadership comes from you. As the leader, you show your team how you own what happens in your business, you take responsibility to fix mistakes and make customers happy. You own what you say, and what you do. Leading like an owner and being held accountable for doing what you say you will do creates an ownership culture in your team and in your downline.

Leading By Example

The next concept is *walking the talk*. The phrase is common enough, but what does it mean for a leader?

It starts with the visible manifestations of what you do: communicating effectively, showing up, acting the way you expect others to act, and generally behaving like a leader. It moves forward to modeling behaviors you want others to emulate:

- Only ask for things you have first demonstrated yourself as willing to do (think before you speak/post, put in the extra effort, do the day-to-day work).

- Watch for say/do gaps. A say/do gap is when you say one thing but do another.

- Set aside your individual needs for the needs of your downline.

Integrating Downline Management With Downline Leadership

It's very important that you integrate the two complementary disciplines of Downline Management and Downline Leadership. By doing so, you achieve the multiplier effect that leads to Downline Success (DS = DM × DL).

As you accelerate your leadership development, you will come across portions of your downline who believe that management is somehow inferior to leadership. **That's not how we see things.** Both disciplines need to be present every day in order for you and your teammates, to drive toward Downline Success.

> "Leadership and management are two distinctive and complementary systems of action... Both are necessary for success in an increasingly complex and volatile business environment."
>
> –John Kotter
>
> What Leaders Really Do (p. 51), 1999
> US Harvard Business Review Book

Downline Leadership works alongside, in concert with, and in balance with Downline Management. Most often, this balance is situational; the effective leader knows when to focus on leading the team and when to focus on the tasks at hand. While striving for that balance, the leader can never forget that it takes both effective Downline Leadership and competent Downline Management to achieve Downline Success.

Let's explore some examples of this integration.

Downline Managers	Downline Leaders	Integrated (DS = DM × DL)
Are attuned to systems and policy	Are attuned to people, emotions, and styles	Are fast, agile, and balanced while focused on success
Solve tactical problems	Resolve strategic challenges	Know when to focus on the tactical issues at hand and when to shift to a strategic viewpoint
Hear the facts and data of the situation	Listen to the emotion and heart of the person	Assess the entire situation with both mind and heart
Focus on short-term results	Build teams with the long term in mind	Deliver both short-term results and long-term positioning

Path Forward: Becoming the Downline Leader

Much of this module was dedicated to exploring the importance of seeing yourself as a leader and developing your leadership capabilities to achieve higher levels of success for you and your team. We looked at being the leader and owner of the downline and how that leads to success. In addition, we explored the Downline Success formula and how to integrate your Downline Management skills with your Downline Leadership competencies.

Now, let's close this module by discussing what it takes to become *that* leader.

It's going to take passion! It's that simple. You already have the insight within you, and this program will help with the development and enhancement of your capabilities. What you have to bring is *passion*—passion to learn, passion to care, and passion to lead.

Downline Leadership is not about mechanics; it's about **meaning**. When things have meaning, you care about them. You care about your teammates, you care about helping others, and you care about achieving success. When these things have meaning to you, it drives your quest for ongoing growth and development.

Remember two of the big questions we asked at the beginning of this module:

- Do you see yourself as a leader?
- Do others see you as a leader?

Your answer may be "No" today, but by the end of this book and program, it will be "Yes"!

Action Required

In preparation for our next group meeting, please complete the following assignment.

Upon Reflection...

Instructions

1. Consider the concepts, ideas, and statements from this module, including how you reacted to them.

2. Use the Discussion Framework as a guide.

3. Capture your preliminary notes, observations, thoughts, and reflections on the next page.

4. When we convene as a group, be prepared to discuss one or more of these frameworks. The group session will help you refine your thoughts and provide you with additional clarity. When you are doing the book alone, it still helps to answer all four questions to really dig into the material from four different perspectives.

Introduction to the Discussion Framework

We use the Discussion Framework to help guide our exploration of each topic. Since this is the first time we are sharing it, this section provides an explanation of how it works.

The framework helps us structure our thoughts on two axes: INTERNAL—EXTERNAL and INDIVIDUAL—GROUP. On the first axis, INTERNAL refers to your inner thoughts and self-awareness, whereas EXTERNAL refers to those that are visible and observable by others. On the other axis, INDIVIDUAL relates to you and GROUP relates to others. You can also replace your TEAM for GROUP if you're doing this book by yourself.

	INTERNAL	EXTERNAL
INDIVIDUAL	REFLECT (*Individual—Internal*) **Inner thoughts** and ideas that are meaningful to you and require **self-awareness**.	ADOPT (*Individual—External*) Relevant actions and behaviors you might take that are visible and observable.
GROUP	INQUIRE (*Group—Internal*) Questions or concerns you have for **the Group (or your team)** to discuss further.	SHARE (*Group—External*) **Actions and behaviors** that you would like to share with the rest of the group (or your team).

Discussion Framework:

Use this page to capture your preliminary thoughts about this module's content. Each quadrant has questions that are provided to help stimulate your thoughts and reflections. This is not a quiz and there are no wrong answers. It's an opportunity to deepen self-awareness, so capture whatever seems appropriate to you.

	INTERNAL	EXTERNAL
INDIVIDUAL	**Reflect** What did you read about this week that caught your eye and caused you to reflect?	**Adopt** What would you like to adopt as a going forward behavior or process that you picked up from this week's module?
GROUP	**Inquire** What questions would you like to ask the group concerning the topic(s) in the module?	**Share** What insight, principle, or leadership precept did you want to share with the group?

LEADERSHIP ENGINE

In the first module, *Downline Leadership*, we spent much of our time having you look inward, assessing who you are as a leader. In this module, we will focus on looking outward, toward other people, while embracing the principle that leadership is fundamentally all about other people and your relationships with them. Developing your Leadership Engine skills will help you connect and engage with your team in an effective and meaningful way.

We define the Leadership Engine as Establishing Credibility, Developing Relationships, Earning Trust, and Gaining Influence with your team and downline. These leadership skills work together to help you build leadership relationships with your team. This module will review how each competency works separately and together.

> Leadership is "influence, nothing more and nothing less."
>
> –John Maxwell
>
> * The 21 Irrefutable Laws of Leadership (p. 11). Nashville, TN: Thomas Nelson. 2007.

If leadership is influence, as Maxwell says, then wouldn't you want to know how to increase your influence? This module helps you to understand how to use the Leadership Engine to do just that: gain influence.

Module Overview

In completing this module, you will

- Explore the Leadership Engine and how it works.
- Review how credibility is the sum of authenticity and believability.
- Discover how you connect with and care for people to build relationships.
- Build your own Relationship Map.
- Investigate how Say/Do alignments are the foundation of trust.
- Find out why influence is not about command and control.
- See why Servant Leaders lead from the bottom.
- Learn how to restore lost relationships and regain trust.

The Leadership Engine

There are four key leadership competencies that work together to produce effective leaders:

- Establishing Credibility
- Developing Relationships
- Earning Trust
- Gaining and Using Influence

These attributes form the Leadership Engine that drives a leader's effectiveness. The engine moves as communication enables each skill.

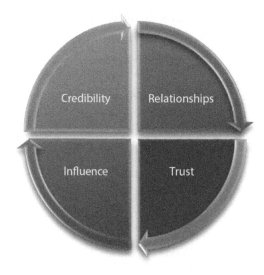

When you first meet someone, you kick-start the engine by triggering the spark of credibility. Once people know who you are and what you stand for, the door is opened to developing a relationship. As you connect with people, listening and relating to them, a relationship is built, and you provide an opening for trust to begin. People trust you when they are confident that you have their back and will be loyal to them. Once they trust you, you are empowered to use your newfound influence with them. Together, you move toward success for you and teammates.

Like pistons in an engine, each element links to and strengthens the next one, using communication to grease the engine, propelling your leadership to operate at higher levels of performance. Let's dig into each of these leadership competencies and the linkages that are formed between them!

What is Credibility?

Credibility is *the quality of being authentic and believable.* While the word credibility itself is fairly well understood, too many leaders believe that their position alone establishes their credibility. **Titles and ranks don't create credibility; leaders must take the initiative to establish credibility with others through their actions and words.** Establishing a foundation of credibility allows for the effective building of relationships. This link to relationships is important to establish when you first engage others and should be nurtured throughout the life of the relationship. Let's explore the cornerstones of credibility.

Authenticity

Being authentic is *being genuine.* Being genuine means you are true to yourself. You have learned to value yourself and others. You are confident, open, trustworthy, and real. Your character and integrity are distinctly apparent. However, caution is advised when contemplating the misleading expression "I'm just being myself." While there is a great deal of truth in that phrase, it can be used as permission for poor behavior or to avoid responsibility for one's actions. It slams the door shut on self-awareness and its crucial role in building powerful credibility.

We prefer a more thoughtful approach to authenticity as "owning one's personal experiences, be they thoughts, emotions, needs, preferences, or beliefs" and behaving in accordance with one's true self.[1]

The power of internal reflection is that it helps us stay authentic to who we are, especially in the fast-paced world most of us inhabit. Think of those times you realized—often too late—that your language, behavior, or interaction was inauthentic. That feeling of "That's not what I meant or who I am as a

---

1   Harter, S. (2002). Authenticity. In C. R. Snyder & S. J. Lopez (Eds.), *Handbook of Positive Psychology* (pp. 382–394). London: Oxford University Press.

person" might be an indicator that you were moving too fast. Mentally slowing down promotes awareness and helps remove obstacles that would otherwise present themselves when moving too quickly.

Another element of authenticity that differentiates it from "just being yourself" is vulnerability. *Authenticity is what happens when honesty meets vulnerability and self-awareness.*

The power of vulnerability is that it reminds you and others that you are human, with all the flaws, mistakes, and imperfections that define it. Vulnerability is the antidote to perfection and promotes an environment of safety that allows connections to happen.

Believability

Whereas authenticity requires a strong level of internal reflection, *believability is what is visible to others.* The drivers for believability are what you've done, what you are doing, and consistency.

What you've done includes your leadership legacy that you left to other people. Your competence is derived from having managed your own business effectively and successfully. Competence is one of the primary ingredients of credibility and drives home that credibility statement of "been there and done that."

However, there's more to believability than being good at the mechanics of managing your business. *Believability is also about how you have related to people in the past, encouraged them, coached them, listened to them, and engaged them.* The extent to which you have established a legacy of leadership will follow you to your next relationship and help you create believability. This allows you to establish credibility with team members individually.

What you are doing refers to what is happening in the moment. Are you fully present and mindful, or are you distracted and distant? Are you interrupting to make your own points, or are you listening intently and reflecting?

Additionally, this dimension of believability is communicated through both verbal and non-verbal mechanisms. Is your confidence coming across, or is your lack of confidence screaming louder than anything? Even more challenging is conveying believability with remote and virtual teams, where communication is cumbersome even with modern technology.

Consistency in words and actions also affects your believability. Because you are in the spotlight, everything you say and do is visible to everyone else. Consistency matters every day and is measured by those around you. A say/do gap chips away at your believability, but when you have say/do alignment, it strengthens your credibility.

Authenticity + Believability = Credibility

When you combine authenticity (how you see yourself) with believability (how others see you), the result is credibility. Now that we've finished our deep dive into credibility, let's move on to Relationships.

What are Relationships?

Relationships are *the way in which people connect to each other*. This fundamental leadership competency is important, not just in terms of the relationships you have with others, but also in your ability to observe, diagnose, and address relationship-related issues and challenges on your team.

Using the credibility you have established allows you to connect readily with people. With solid credibility established, connections drive deeper between each person in the relationship. Using different forms of connection enables you to build distinctive relationships with each individual. As each relationship grows, the foundation for trust is being created. People see your character and integrity through interaction and work and begin to link credibility and relationship to the element of trust.

Relationships occur through the combination of *caring* and *connecting*. When you care about a person and truly connect with them, you foster a relationship with that individual.

Caring

To build a relationship, *you need to care about the other person, including their goals, viewpoints, and needs.* When you care about that person in a visible and real way, they know it. Furthermore, when they know you care, it establishes the emotional foundation that allows a relationship to flourish.

> *"People don't care how much you know until they know how much you care."*
>
> –Theodore Roosevelt

Caring happens at the person-to-person level, making it vital to focus on each specific individual. *Caring for someone means respecting who he or she is, what that person stands for, and what he or she values.* What's important to them becomes important to you.

Caring for someone means committing to them and their goals. When they reach those goals, you show that you care about them when you recognize them for those achievements.

Caring gives them a sense of safety and belonging. They gain perspective on who they are and where they fit in. As a result, their relationship with you is strengthened.

Implicit in all of this is that you are listening. You ask a person questions and genuinely hear what they are saying. If you care, you will listen. There will be more on listening in the "Communication" module.

Connecting

If *caring* is the emotion behind building relationships, then *connecting* is the action. Connection occurs when you have fostered a two-way form of communication that is mutual, trusted, and effective. Accordingly, a relationship grows through various acts of connection. The challenge is to be able to connect with each person at deeper levels than you have before.

Each person is unique and can come from various generations, global environments, or cultural backgrounds. Accordingly, each person requires a creative and special connection to build a relationship.

To grow your ability to make connections, you need to exercise and stretch yourself. The next time you meet a new person (or an existing friend), attempt a new approach to expand your connection. If you've only asked surface questions about the other person's background, try asking deeper questions that uncover more of who they are as a person. If you tend to speak too much, try to listen more.

Acknowledgement and Recognition

One of the most powerful ways to build relationships and yet one commonly missed leadership act is to acknowledge the contribution of a teammate and to say a simple "thank you." It's all too easy to just go about your job, track the tasks, and move ahead when someone does their job. **But what type of leadership legacy are you leaving if you never acknowledge accomplishments?** As long as the acknowledgement is proportional to the task, you should make sure you celebrate it. These simple and frequently small actions of acknowledgement bear significant fruit with your team.

Likeability

Lastly, it helps if you're just plain likable when building relationships. Here is an excellent list of traits of likeable people from Kathy Caprino ("How to Increase Your Likability in 2015 [And Beyond]," *Forbes Magazine*, 12/12/2014):

- They relate open-heartedly to others.
- They're kind and gentle, not critical.
- They are able to walk in another's shoes.
- They have a ready laugh and easy sense of humor.
- They don't take themselves too seriously.
- They have high integrity and generate trust easily.
- They seem genuinely happy to be in their own skin and to relate to others from a place of confidence.
- They are grateful for what they have and who they are.
- They're happy for other people's success and joy.

Relationship Map

It is critical that leaders see the need to be proactive and strategic in building, developing, and managing relationships. To assist you in being strategic, we suggest two exercises as part of our tool called the "Relationship Map."

First, we ask you to identify what we call the "Three Circles." This doesn't have to be complicated. Simply make 3 different lists:

1. Inner Circle: the 3-5 people that make or break your life. This could include your spouse or partner, children, and a few close friends.

2. Your Business Builders – the people who make or break your business. These are your most engaged, active people you work with on a

frequent basis that influence the momentum results of your team. (Please don't list every business builder; select perhaps 3-20 max)

3. Your Rising Superstars – this is the most exciting category! Look throughout your entire team, and identify 3-5 new or early business builders, in any leg and at any level... the ones with a spark and fire in them. These are your future Diamonds and the ones you want to work with purposely over the course of the next 10-12 weeks. The plan would be for you to intentionally pour into them through educating, mentoring, and coaching. Working with new leaders is a way to keep things fresh and exciting for you, and keep you connected to the basics of business building, as well as a way to really help new folks get off to a great start!

Next, take these three groups of people and plug them into a "Relationship Map." This tool can be a simple matrix where the people are the rows and the columns are different areas of a relationship that a leader may want to track for their team. Both the rows and the columns are customizable by you, should address those things you consider important in building relationships, and denote with whom the relationship is built. Some common relationship areas to consider for your columns are:

- Personality styles (Color, DISC, Meyer-Briggs)
- Love Language

- Communication styles/needs
- Likes to lead from in front or from behind
- Social circles
- Commitment level
- Potential Business Builder
- Jumps In/Needs Help

- Overall emotional health
- Level of risk they can handle
- Social interaction needs
- Flexibility
- Collaboration skills
- Dominant mood

- Hot buttons

- Micro vs. Macro management

- Who talks to whom; where are the informal networks?
- Their level of influence on the team
- How they come to agreement
- Overall health of the relationship
- Strengths
- Biggest Block
- What interdependent goals do you have with this person?
- What motivates them?
- What turns them off?
- How do they like to be recognized?
- Current Rank or level within business
- Annual Goal
- BHAG—Big Hairy Audacious Goal; end goal
- Business Building Plan

- Listener vs. talker

- Takes action or delegates

- Relationship Goal (Build, Grow, Nurture, Maintain)

- Relationship Strategy (How are you going to build this relationship?)

*Note: if you are a part of our official Downline Leadership 10-week coaching groups through www.buildingupleaders.com, your coach will provide you with an editable template of the Relationship Map; you don't need to create it yourself! If you're reading this book on your own without a Certified Building Up Leaders® coach, use the list above to create a personalized Excel spreadsheet with the categories that are most important to you. We suggest that you create 3 different sheets, one for each group, as each group may have different columns/questions/attributes.

Being intentional, purposeful, and proactive about your relationships will almost always pay off in huge dividends. You're probably wondering, "How do I fill out this Relationship Map?" Here are a couple of tips:

- How do I choose the people?
  - o Simple, just follow the instructions above for the three groups
- How do I choose which columns to go with?
  - o Pick the columns that are relevant to the group
  - o Pick the columns that are important to you
  - o Pick the columns that will help you to achieve the relationships you want
  - o The best columns tend to be created by you
- How do I get the answers for each cell?
  - o Fill the form out yourself
  - o Ask the other person, be genuine
  - o Have a group meeting
  - o Use your intuition in each column to determine when you want outside input

The two most important columns are the last two: Relationship Goal and Relationship Strategy/Plan.

- Choose the right Relationship Goal for each person
  - o Build—for those new relationships where you are just beginning and need to get to know the other person.

- o Grow—you want to really expand and deepen the relationship. Be sure you prioritize these, because you can't grow every relationship you have.

- o Nurture—this relationship has had a gap materialize and you need to work to bridge the gap.

- o Maintain—normal choice for some of your older relationships that still need an investment of time and energy to keep the relationship alive.

- Customize the Relationship Strategy by letting the goal drive the components of your relationship plan

  - o Building usually requires frequent interaction with lots of discussion across a myriad of topics.

  - o Growing usually requires deeper discussions.

  - o Nurturing usually requires reaching out with empathy.

  - o Maintaining usually requires reassurance of loyalty and lots of memories.

Credibility done. Relationships covered. Trust is up next!

What is Trust?

Trust is defined as *the reliance on a person's integrity, ability, and character.* Trust is a sacred pact where we place our faith and confidence in someone, believing that they will perform a future task in a way that is consistent with what they have declared about themselves. Said another way—*you believe that they will do what they say they will do.*

When you have established a foundation of credibility and developed a relationship, you have cultivated the soil in which trust can flourish. One of the challenges in today's world of constant change is to earn trust as soon as possible. For leaders, the goal is to achieve "Trusted Advisor" status, where the level of commitment is high and the link to influence is activated.

The typically dynamic nature of relationships makes earning trust particularly important and challenging. It can take a long time for trust to build, requiring a cycle of commitment and execution that repeats several times. Unfortunately, it can take only a moment in time for trust to be broken.

Let's further consider how trust is the glue of relationships and the foundation that leads to influence.

Trust bonds relationships

Relationships are tied together by bonds made up of a series of links and connections. Trust strengthens those bonds. With trust, the interactions and connectivity you have with people tend to be more fruitful, effective, and fulfilling.

- As trust is earned, people feel safer and more empowered to speak out. Their communications are more productive and less restricted as they articulate their thoughts without fear of retribution.

- The more trust you have with someone, the more you can extend yourself and be transparent. Interactions between you become increasingly deeper and more open, as well as more proactive, when trust is present.

- Trust helps to achieve a shared vision and common commitment. The more trust is present, the less need there is for check-ins, and the more likely it is that people will speak up if something begins to track away from the vision.

- Trust is always personal. There are times that the leader will put their reputation on the line because they "trust" someone. If that trust is broken, it hurts—sometimes deeply. See the section on "When the Engine Fails" later in this module to address this situation.

Let's review the unique aspects of how trust is established and grown.

Earning Trust

Trust is earned; it doesn't happen any other way. The cycle of "you trust them, they trust you" starts and ends with you. You must be competent, honest, a clear communicator, and able to connect with people and do what you say you will do to earn their trust. You also need to be the one to take the initiative in establishing trust.

It Starts With You

The first opportunity starts with you, as early as the first meeting between you and the other person. During the early stages of the relationship, you have the opportunity to earn trust by clearly articulating your personal message. Share with them who you are, how you operate, your desire to listen, and what your passion is.

Frequently, to earn trust with others, you must trust them first. Extending trust means taking a risk. Trust can't be achieved without taking a risk, and you can't reap the benefits of trust without stepping out. It's not easy, taking that first step to trust your teammates, especially before they have proven themselves. **Giving out trust gives them the chance to earn it!**

The Cycle Continues and Repeats

The basic principle of the trust cycle is that it keeps going as long as trust continues to be strengthened through successful say/do activities. You trust someone and they receive your trust and act on it. As they are successful, trust is returned back to you, strengthened. The roles reverse on a frequent basis to grow the trust levels between you.

Becoming a Trusted Advisor

As your level of trust increases with someone, you reach a level of "Trusted Advisor" in their eyes. You can't force the trusted advisor role to happen, but you can continue growing the level of trust with someone until they determine you have become that trusted advisor to them.

When you are the trusted advisor, others will

- Seek your advice.
- Engage with you on strategic issues.
- Communicate with you more freely.
- Involve you earlier in important discussions.
- Support your decisions and judgment.
- Be more easily influenced by you.

You've worked on credibility, relationships, and trust—now on to influence!

What is Influence?

Influence is *the ability to affect a person's behavior in the direction of success*. Influence is a relationship-oriented function and is associated with people and your dealings with them. Influence can be **seen** when you motivate and encourage another person. Influence can be **felt** when you inspire a person to action. Influence can be **heard** when you are the voice and driving force behind their growth as a leader.

All the elements of effective relationship building enhance your ability to gain and use influence. Successful use of influence strengthens relationships, expands trust, and increases your credibility. When you can effectively influence the team and the customer, you are able to lead them to success.

Through effective communication, your influence with the team grows and goals are achieved. The leadership engine races even faster. Your link to credibility now comes full circle at a higher and more effective level, and the cycle continues.

While these descriptions of influence focus on what you do, in reality, *influence is all about the other person and how you interact with that person*. In the end, your ability to have influence is a result of building and strengthening your relationships with others.

Before explaining further what influence is and how to intentionally use it, let's clarify what influence is *not*.

Influence is Not About Command and Control, Authority, or Positional Power

Real influence isn't achieved through control. You can get things accomplished using control, but leaders find that using control is a limited form of execution that doesn't last long. Controlling someone and not allowing the free will of decision-making leads to frustration, disengagement, and disempowerment. Having genuine influence means that you are enabled to motivate and inspire people to greatness.

Some leaders assume that their position and authority are all that are needed to make people do what they want. Positional leadership is closely related to "control," and is the *least effective method of leadership*. Resentment builds as the team's ideas continue not to be heard. Leaders who are stuck in this mode see the power and prestige of their position as the reason they should be entitled to influence, but it doesn't work that way. From a leadership perspective, control is short-term and influence is long-term.

Influence is also not persuasion. Persuasion is when you try to convince someone to take an action after arguing your case. This means appealing to them through either logic or emotion, and trying to get them to make a decision in your direction. However, it's not using your relationship and trust to influence them; it feels like you have manipulated them instead.

Influence is certainly **not** coercion. When you coerce someone through force or threats, they only take action because they are afraid of the consequences of not acting. This doesn't strengthen the relationship—it weakens it, and in the end they either rebel against you or leave.

What does influence need to work?

People need to see your character and your integrity in order for you to be in a position to influence them. They have to see you as honest and understanding and as you truly caring about them as a person. How do you build influence?

- Build your influence by using the Leadership Engine (Credibility, Relationships, Trust).

- Strengthen and use your influence on a regular basis.

- Empower the other person to build their own influence.

Using the Leadership Engine to build relationships has been explained previously in the Credibility, Relationships, and Trust sections of this module.

To strengthen and use your influence on a regular basis, begin by finding alignment between what's important to the person and their goals. This enables you to find opportunities to engage your influence to strengthen the person and achieve greater results from your leadership. As more results occur, their trust for you continues to grow. While this cycle can occasionally have setbacks, in general, your influence grows each time the cycle of trust, influence, and results are achieved.

Lastly, as you use your influence with people over and over again toward success, they see firsthand how influence works. The door is then opened for you to invest in them and help them build their own influence. This creates a leadership legacy of developing other leaders. They use what they have seen you model to build credibility, develop relationships, earn trust, and gain influence with others.

Servant Leadership

Influence is a powerful element of leadership. As such, it needs to be respected, handled with care, and approached with a humble attitude. An effective way to do this is to see yourself as a Servant Leader.

A Servant Leader sees the typical leadership pyramid as an inverted one, with the team at the top and the leader at the bottom. This helps change the management perspective from "the team is to serve the leader's needs" to a servant leadership perspective where "the leader is to serve the needs of the team." **This paradigm shift changes everything!** The focus now moves entirely to the team and away from you. You have the opportunity to use your influence to help the team, develop them, encourage them, and inspire them to success.

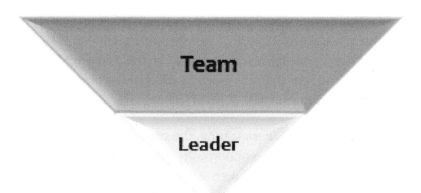

Critically important to making the Servant Leader role work is the active presence of humility in everything the Servant Leader does. *A Servant Leader introduces their team first, they strive to understand the team's needs first, and they seek to hear the team's input before voicing their own.* When the team sees this consistent focus on them and not on the Servant Leader, the team opens up to the influence of the leader. The Servant Leader can then take up the mantle of leader and motivator.

A Servant Leader will utilize the role of *Coach* to pull the best out of their team and get collaborative solutions and insight into how to overcome the challenges. A coach helps the person or team solve their own problems by asking open-ended questions. In fact, it is so important that the Servant Leader be a coach that we highly suggest that they use the "coach-first" approach, seeing every situation as an opportunity to *ask questions first*. This shows genuine respect and care for the team. We will discuss the role of coach in much greater length in the "Coaching" module.

The Leadership Engine is complete! But what happens if it breaks down?

When the Engine Fails

Relationships are hard. They can fail, trust can be broken, and either side can be hurt. They can be difficult to grow, nurture, and cultivate once a breakdown has occurred. What do we do to restore the relationship if it fails or if trust is broken?

Restoring Relationships

There will be times when your relationship with someone on the team suffers, either due to a mistake you made or to a misunderstanding. While there are some breaks that cannot be restored, many can be. Amazingly, like a broken bone that heals stronger than the original, often the relationship is not only restored, but also strengthened.

It's important that, in a business setting, the situation of losing a relationship with a customer be seen as an opportunity. Many stories have been written of relationships having been broken with a customer for lousy service or inadequate products only to be reversed by amazing service or incredible products. The secret is to *take immediate action when the relationship is broken*. The longer the relationship struggles, the harder it will be to reverse. Apologize, assure them it will NEVER happen again, don't make excuses, and don't pass the buck. Do whatever it takes to right the wrong.

With teammates, the dynamics can be different from those of a customer. For example, how do you recover from an incident where you talked about someone behind their back and they found out? While the first action is the same—you apologize and assure them it will never happen again—the second action is to customize your relationship-building action to meet the needs of the hurt party. Perhaps you can become a public advocate for the team member instead of a private detractor. Assuming this is the right action to take, you can actually turn the relationship around and rebuild the person's confidence and trust in you.

When you see your relationships as *investments*, you desire to have a return on your investment. Make the effort, figure out what went wrong, make it right, and *move on, together.*

Broken Trust

Another example of when the engine fails is when someone breaks trust. The sad truth is that there will be an incident where someone you trust doesn't follow through, and trust is broken. It happens to everyone, and when you think about it, you've broken trust with someone yourself. So, what do you do?

First, meet with the other person and uncover *why* the trust was not honored. Often there is a solid explanation for the lack of follow-through, and likely there had not been an adequate setting of expectations or effective communication before or after the event. Put a plan in place to help mediate the situation and shore up the communication links. This will likely go a long way toward restoring the relationship.

What if it was something serious, something callous, or the other person just didn't care? Begin as above: Meet with them to uncover why the task wasn't completed, then take on the coach role. Ask open-ended questions to obtain the background behind the lack of follow through. Perhaps it was something you had done, or not done, a long time ago that was held against you. Dig deep and find out where the other person is coming from. Then, focus on how their actions (or lack thereof) hurt themselves, the team, or the customer. Bring them back into the fabric of the team and plan together for recovery. Plan something small to help them regain momentum. Fulfill the original miss, preferably with them directly involved, and measure progress more frequently, offering help or clarification when necessary.

What if YOU were the one who betrayed someone else's trust? First and foremost, you must acknowledge that trust was broken and admit to your role. Then, apologize. It doesn't matter what the mitigating circumstances were; you need to own up to the miss and apologize in a genuine and heartfelt way. Then assess the new/current situation and start over. Only with true ownership of your own miss can you reset expectations and gain new buy-in on the task. Work hard to rebuild their trust. Warn them immediately if you encounter a new problem or hurdle. Over-communicate, as it's an important time to make sure everything is covered.

A little more on those pesky say/do gaps that so often are the cause of broken trust. There are two primary drivers of say/do gaps: overcommitting on your say and lack of clarity on your say. Too often we commit to people that we will do something, only to find out we have committed to be somewhere else at the same time. The simple solution is to make MUCH fewer commitments, then fight tooth and nail to meet those commitments. Instead of fifty commitments this week, start with just five! Truly trustworthy people are generally people who make few commitments, and never miss. The other driver is when you commit to do something but there is a lack of clarity and specificity as to what you committed to do. Even if you get it done, no one is sure if you did. "I'm going to help you with the next class." What does that actually mean? Are you committing to being at the next class? Are you committing to teaching all or part of the class? No one actually knows, and hence a say/do gap is created. Try to ensure that you both agree to exactly what is being committed to.

If you can fully recover from broken trust, you may find that the relationship can go to a deeper level than before! It's worth the effort.

Time for another story!

Comeback!

Liz enrolled Shawnte over three months ago. Everything started smoothly at the beginning as Liz had shared her story with Shawnte and it really helped her to make a decision to buy a kit and start the business. After that first series of interactions, the relationship slowed down a lot and Liz hadn't had any solid discussions with Shawnte for two months.

Liz was pretty busy with her other businesspeople and admittedly didn't do a great job keeping in touch with Shawnte, so she wasn't that surprised when Shawnte contacted her looking for some help. Liz didn't have a lot of time that morning, so her note to Shawnte was a little brief, but Liz figured that her relationship with Shawnte would be more than enough to cover the note. She justified it to herself by thinking, "I mean, I just didn't have the time, and I was hustling out the door." Liz didn't hear from Shawnte for over a week, and Liz forgot to follow up with Shawnte.

A month later, Liz was shocked! Shawnte sent a note simply saying that she was leaving the business, wished Liz the best, and there was no need to get back to her.

How was this possible? How did this happen? Liz's first reaction was to get mad at Shawnte and call her immature. Then Liz took a breath and reflected on the relationship. It wasn't pretty. When Liz looked at how she had really not been there for Shawnte for two months, then let a busy morning and lack of follow-up trash the relationship, she went from mad to sad.

*Time for action! Liz didn't write a note this time—she called Shawnte directly. Liz had messed up, and this was going to be a humbling experience. Instead of dancing around the topic, Liz immediately apologized to Shawnte. She **didn't make any excuses or give explanations**; just simply said she was sorry and asked if she could talk to Shawnte next week at her earliest convenience about how to help her. Liz was sincere, humble, apologetic, and caring. Shawnte said OK and they ended up having a great conversation the following week.*

Shawnte decided to stay in the business, and while she hasn't hit Silver yet, her business is making consistent progress, and her relationship with Liz... solid as a rock now. That's what Liz calls a comeback!

Discussion

Liz had several chances to build this relationship. Why do you think she didn't take the time? What would you have done differently? Liz seemed to do a great job of recovery; what do you think of her actions to restore the relationship? What would you be doing now to continue to grow the relationship?

The Path Forward

In this module, we introduced the Leadership Engine, which starts with Credibility and moves on to Relationships, Trust, and Influence. Understanding the linkages between these elements helps you gain maximum impact from each and enjoy the whole engine, which is greater than the sum of the parts.

Additionally, we dug into each of the four leadership competencies:

- Credibility = Authenticity + Believability

- Relationships require you to connect with and care about people.

- Trust is all about your integrity and character, and the ability to do what you say you will do.

- Influence moves people without controlling or directing them.

The Leadership Engine is all about the relationships you have with people. Even when those relationships are strained, the Engine helps you recover. Lastly, it is with humility and a spirit of servanthood that leaders make a real difference.

Action Required

In preparation for our next group meeting, please fill out the Discussion Framework on the next page.

Discussion Framework:

Use this page to capture your preliminary thoughts about this module's content. Each quadrant has questions that are provided to help stimulate your thoughts and reflection. This is not a quiz, and there are no wrong answers. It is an opportunity to deepen self-awareness, so capture whatever seems appropriate to you.

	INTERNAL	EXTERNAL
INDIVIDUAL	**Reflect** What did you read about this week that caught your eye and caused you to reflect? _____ _____ _____ _____ _____	**Adopt** What would you like to adopt as a going forward behavior or process that you picked up from this week's module? _____ _____ _____ _____ _____
GROUP	**Inquire** What question would you like to ask the group concerning the topic(s) in the module? _____ _____ _____ _____ _____	**Share** What insight, principle, or leadership precept did you want to share with the group? _____ _____ _____ _____ _____

COMMUNICATION

Communication is the method by which people interact with each other and transfer information. Sounds pretty cold, right? That's because that short description is missing the emotional connection that takes place during effective communication. Let's try that again: **Communication is listening, caring, sharing, and connecting with the other person, your team, and downline.**

To truly communicate, you have to dig deep and gain a full understanding of the emotion and intentions behind the words. Effective communication involves two-way interaction. It requires you to have insight into the message you have sent, as well as into how that message is received. For example: What did the other person hear you say? What was their emotional response to your message? How did you respond?

More than just the words you use, effective communication means experiencing true emotions. Emotionally intelligent communication is all about trying to see things from the other person's perspective. Effective communication helps you deepen your connections to your team and downline. It also enables you to have difficult conversations without destroying trust.

Module Overview

In completing this module, you will:

- Review the relationship between connection and communication.
- Explore ways to increase your effectiveness while speaking and listening.
- Determine the best approach to writing your message.
- Discover how to evaluate if your message was felt.

Communication is Connection

Why communicate at all? Put simply, it's to connect with people. Our lives—and hopefully theirs—are enriched when we connect with others.

What does connecting mean? Connecting is that moment when you *get* what the other person is saying or writing. You are drawn closer to each other through the experience of communicating. We'll discuss different forms of communicating, but first, here are a few more ideas on how to connect with others from *The 21 Irrefutable Laws of Leadership* by John Maxwell:[2]

You have to connect with yourself first

Downline Leadership is all about raising your self-awareness, then relating to others. It becomes difficult to connect with others when you don't know who *you* are.

Communicate with openness and sincerity

Be genuine and real. Show them that you care about them and their goals.

Live your message

Be accountable to yourself for what you say and what you expect of others.

Go to where they are

It's difficult to relate to people from behind your private message or text. Try to meet with others in person whenever possible.

Work harder on remote teams

Generally, it takes more time, effort, creativity, and strategy to build relationships with virtual teams, especially if they are from a different culture or country. Don't let anyone dissuade you, though! No matter where someone is from, they are still just people, and you *can* connect with them!

Focus on them, not yourself

Pay REAL attention to them. Be present and in the moment when you are together. Be mindful of what matters to them and seek to discover the ways in which they want to interact with you.

---

2   pp. 117-119. Nashville, TN: Thomas Nelson. 2007.

Offer direction and hope

When speaking with them, be a source of help, direction, and hope. Be an encourager, showing genuine interest in their challenges and their decisions.

Now that we have touched on connecting, let's move on to what it means to connect on a personal level.

Connecting on a Personal Level

To really establish relationships, you have to go past shallow online discussions and spend time talking with people. Find your balance between the time you spend writing to someone and the time you spend speaking to them.

Here is a short example list, in priority order, of communication methods. Let's explore where you invest your communication time and the effectiveness of each method. After this, we'll contrast speaking and writing.

- **Face-to-Face:** Nothing beats relationship development through face-to-face meetings! Nothing! You get the full spectrum of interaction and engagement. This should be your top goal whenever possible for spending time with someone. However, you can't always meet, so...

- **Video conference:** Zoom, FaceTime, Skype, Marco Polo and other video apps should be your second option. Not quite the same as face-to-face, but you will find it is still better than a regular phone call. You get all of the physical cues and you see people's eyes when they speak. We also recommend that you use this approach with groups when you can.

- **Phone calls:** Still one of our go-to ways to spend time with people is to use the phone. You hear their voice, their inflection, and their laughter. You can have intimate discussions and engage in real-time problem solving.

- **Private Message/Text Message:** These two are not exactly the same, but pretty close. In today's world, this form of communication comes before an email. It's still almost real-time and allows for certain personal touches to bring the parties closer to each other. This form is quickly becoming today's standard for quick and tight communication, and you need to master the shortcuts, acronyms, and emoticons that can make it more effective.

- **Email:** Email helps when communicating things of importance that need to be structured or recorded, like action items, upcoming schedules, commitments, attachments, etc. Unfortunately, it doesn't help with having real conversations, which is at the heart of communication, and many people today do not use email.

- **Mail:** Snail mail should be used very sparingly, but if done in a creative manner, it can still elicit amazing results. Using mail for gifts, unexpected surprises, and short cards remains a wonderful idea.

Speaking and Listening

Everyone talks and listens; it's a major form of communication. Let's start with listening, as that's where many of us fall short.

Listening

Effective listening can make all the difference in communication and connecting!

By this point in your life, you've read books about how to listen, you've completed exercises, and you've practiced. Yet no matter how advanced you are, there is always room for improvement. Listening effectively takes effort, focus, and concentration.

Listening is an intensive activity! You have to pay attention to what is being *said*, as well as to what is being *communicated*. Sometimes, those are very different things.

> *"The most basic of all human needs is the need to understand and be understood. The best way to understand people is to listen to them."*
>
> –Ralph Nichols

Even though the following list of listening tips includes some fundamentals, they can be beneficial to review while thinking about your own effectiveness in each.

- Listen intently. Try to understand what people are really saying, not just what you hear.
  - Listen to *their* words instead of thinking about what you are going to say next. The goal is to listen, not merely respond.

- o Be curious; have an inquiry-based mindset.
- o If you don't know why they are saying something, ask instead of making assumptions.
- Make the other person your singular focus.
  - o Eliminate distractions. In today's interruption-driven world, giving someone your full and undivided attention can be the greatest display of care and empathy you can offer.
  - o Value what they are saying. Don't just collect information or data. Realize that there is a serious reason for them to be speaking to you, not just a casual thought.
  - o Don't pass judgment on what they are saying. Don't qualify it, categorize it, or label it—just let them be the center of your universe for the time they are speaking.
  - o Seek first to understand before trying to be understood.
- Be a coach when listening.
  - o Ask open-ended questions as you are talking with them, and then listen to the answers. Open-ended questions reveal the "why" in their thoughts.
  - o Don't try to solve their problem. Use your open-ended questions to help *them* solve their own issue.
  - o Allow for silence. If they stop talking, relax and wait, don't jump at the chance for "your turn." Sometimes the most valuable things are said after a silent pause. They are evaluating your listening status and determining whether to continue confiding in and connecting with you further.
- Be a good observer when others are talking.
  - o You can learn a lot by observing others interact. Does one person interrupt too often? How does the other person feel when that happens?
  - o If you need to channel your energy, write down your questions, statements, or thoughts! When you normally would interrupt, write things down and keep listening instead. See what happens.

Listening helps you connect to others and can be used to help others effectively connect to each other.

Speaking

Here's our goal when we speak: **Say the right thing, at the right time, to the right person, in the right way.** A pretty lofty goal for sure, but when achieved, you've connected with the other person(s) through your spoken words. Let's focus on two major types of speaking: One-on-One and Groups.

One-on-One Conversations

It's so important for you to be real and genuine when speaking with someone on a one-to-one basis. There is nowhere to hide; who you are will be very evident to the other person. Here are a few tips for your conversation:

- **Eye contact**—Make eye contact and exude warmth when you meet the other person.

- **Names**—Study beforehand the name of the other person, even practicing how to say it. Remember their name and connect it to their face.

- **Look your best**—Prepare yourself to be presentable and portray the image you want each time you meet with the other person.

- **Be on time**—Get there early and be prepared to stay late. Plan ahead for traffic, room conflicts, and phone problems. Always be on time!

- **Watch your body language**—Smile and be warm, attentive, and focused. Your body language will reflect the thoughts you have about the dialogue and the other person. Make sure they are positive; if they're not, your body *will* give you away.

- **Keep it positive**—When you are meeting the other person, be positive, confident, competent, and capable. The positive impression you give will be worth its weight in gold as the other person receives this "can-do" impression of you right from the start.

- **Pay attention**—Listen, listen, listen! Make sure the other person knows you are paying attention to every word they are saying. Use your active listening skills. Ask for feedback, engage them, respect what they have to say, and ask open-ended questions.

- **Be yourself**—Remember to relax and just be yourself—that's whom they want to meet. The other person may be uncomfortable meeting you. It's up to you to be genuine and real and to help them relax.

Before we move onto speaking to groups, let's take a moment to focus on a particular one-on-one conversation that needs some added attention: The Crucial/Difficult Conversation.

Crucial Conversations

A crucial (commonly known as difficult) conversation is *a discussion between two or more people where (1) stakes are high, (2) opinions vary, and (3) emotions run strong.* This discussion is something that needs to happen when you have a disagreement or challenge with someone.

The authors of *Crucial Conversations* detail the following seven steps to have a difficult conversation:[3]

1. **Start with Heart**—Examine your motives. What do you really want from the conversation, and what is at stake? You have to ask yourself these questions to determine how important this conversation is to you and the other person. Put your heart out there and be genuine.

2. **Learn to Look**—Always look at the conversation as it unfolds. The question to be asked is "How are we communicating? Are we hearing and understanding eachother?" Be on the lookout for a lack of mutual purpose. Protect your conversation from going downhill with an "I think we've moved away from our dialogue" or "I'm sorry. I've been trying to force my ideas on you."

3. **Make it Safe**—When you notice that the conversation has moved away from safe dialogue, do something to make it more comfortable. Ask a question and show interest in others' views. Apologies, smiles, even a request for a brief time-out can help restore safety when things get dicey.

4. **Master your Story**—We tell ourselves stories that may make us the villain, the victim, or a totally helpless observer. People jump to false conclusions based on the stories they tell themselves. Focus on your true story, and tell yourself that story over and over again before having the crucial conversation.

5. **STATE your Path**—**S**hare your facts; **T**ell your story; **A**sk for the other person's path; **T**alk with empathy; and **E**ncourage open-ended

---

3   Kerry Patterson, Joseph Crenny, Ron McMillan, and Al Switzler. 2003.

questions. This is the heart of the conversation: sharing each other's story. Do this in a way that will make the other party feel safe telling their story as well.

6. **Explore Others' Paths**—A dialogue allows you to actively inquire about the other's views. Now that you both understand each other, you can emphasize which parts you agree upon and the areas in which you differ.

7. **Move to Action**—Come to a shared decision about what will happen, then settle on a way to follow up and document it. This fosters accountability and responsibility.

That was a great list from the authors of *Crucial Conversations*. Here's another set of practical tips for getting ready for a crucial conversation:

- Get over your anger and hurt, and find a peaceful place before the meeting. Assume positive intentions and outcomes will result from the discussion.

- Have a clear plan and purpose before the discussion. Get clear on your goals for the conversation as well as any potential limiting beliefs, triggers, or things you need to be aware of beforehand.

- Be empathetic with the other person's situation or circumstance.

- Make sure that the dialogue is grounded in facts before exploring emotions.

- Ask open-ended questions (in the right tone).

- Make sure your tone is personal and direct, but not attacking or aggressive in nature.

- Have the conversation sooner rather than later, but you may need to let a little time go by to let emotions settle down (up to 24 hours).

- Find common ground.

- Don't retreat, even if you didn't know all the facts. There was a reason you wanted the meeting in the first place, so don't give up on your intention.

Being able to have crucial conversations as part of your skill set means you increase your chances of connecting with the other person. **In the end, you have to go with your gut and what you believe is right.** These discussions are about developing, enhancing, and sometimes salvaging relationships. If the relationships weren't important to you, then there would be little purpose in having the discussion. Focus on the other person and do everything you can to reach them without sacrificing your integrity.

There is obviously a lot to reflect on about one-on-one discussions. What skills are needed when speaking to a group?

Speaking to a group

A Downline Leader seeks to connect to others in the room and hold their attention as needed. This discussion is for in-person presentations, but most of this also applies to Facebook Live and webinars.

Here are some behaviors that will help you connect to a group:

- Acknowledge everyone in the room and use their group name (or individual names if possible) in an authentic manner.

- Be clear and *proportional* in your communication. Proportional means understanding the level of detail that is needed at that moment.

- Have confidence during your presentation:
  o Maintain eye contact when in person.
  o Monitor your volume and vocalization, especially for remote participants.
  o Be naturally expressive.

- Empathize with the people in the room.

- Keep the meeting on track.

- Ask for help when appropriate.

- Engage the group with professionalism and transparency.

- Draw in and engage the meeting participants at a high level.

Admittedly, we don't always have a chance to connect with everyone on the team to build credibility and relationships prior to meeting them. So how can we do it in the moment and on the spot? **Confidence.** People connect with you when you exhibit confidence in your body language, in your voice, and in your delivery. Bring your authentic self—based on solid information and awareness of the situation you are in—and show your commitment to connecting with the group.

Presence and the Present

Connecting to groups requires you to be present. This is more than just being in the room. Presence can be defined as the singular focus to the very moment you are in, the discussion going on, the person you are with, and the emotions being expressed. The key here is *the present* moment. It does little good to catch things on your mental replay as you distance yourself from the situation. You need to show up and bring absolutely all of your attention to bear. This principle also applies to your one-on-one discussions.

The more present you are, the more information you receive from the room. It increases your internal and external levels of awareness and allows you to *feel* what is going on. You are able to listen in a way that encourages people to talk and to say what they really think. All of this means that your intuition is kicked into high gear and you can read the room and its participants.

The higher the stakes of any meeting or exchange, the harder mindfulness becomes. Worrying about what could happen—what something might mean days or weeks down the road—can divert anyone's attention from the most important raw input: what's going on in the room at that moment.

When you are focused on the present moment and have a clear vision of your ultimate goal, you will be your most influential and effective.

Body Language

Think of a leader. Better yet, go and look at any memorial statue of a famous person. The style of sculpture may be different, but the body language is always the same. It doesn't change across cultures or over time; the same set of postures, poses, and mannerisms have conveyed confidence and strength since the dawn of time. Body language is part of the core operating system of human communication.

If you carry yourself as a leader, people assume on an instinctive level that you *are* a leader.

Body language is so fundamental that adopting strong postures can give you confidence even when you don't have any. Furthermore, if you hold yourself like you are unafraid, it is almost impossible for anyone to know otherwise.

Here are a few other tips to think about:

- When appropriate, stand.

- Spine straight, shoulders back.

- Don't fidget or pace.

- Be free and comfortable with hand gestures.

- SMILE!

- Make eye contact.

- For remote, phone-based interactions, your presence is primarily conveyed by your voice. Be highly mindful of your cadence, pitch, inflection, tempo, and volume. Smile even while on the phone. It comes through in your voice.

Lastly, how you dress has a powerful psychological effect on your audience. If nothing else, the way you dress demonstrates how much you care. If you dress in a way that makes you feel comfortable, confident, and impactful, the rest will follow naturally.

Know your Audience

Demonstrating confidence, courage, and command of the topic in a way that is visible to others requires knowing when and with whom to communicate, as well as being aware of the audience and the ability to adapt accordingly.

We all have a limited amount of attention. Some research has indicated that for in-person meetings, any topic that lasts more than 10-18 minutes will cause people to lose focus; for virtual or phone meetings, the time can be even less. The more time that you spend worrying about yourself (a natural and logical thing to do when you are standing in front of people), the less time you have to be aware of what's going on with other people and focus on them.

In person, it's easy to overcome honest mistakes, but it's very difficult to recover if you are not paying attention to the people in the room.

Differences between speaking and writing

As we leave the topic of speaking to begin covering the topic of writing, it's appropriate to identify two major differences between the two topics you need to be aware of:

Repetition

When speaking, repetition can help to drive home an important point. Because of the nature of listening, it's up to you, the speaker, to state, remind, refresh, and hammer home a point as the audience is going through many thoughts and possible distractions while you are speaking. When writing, however, repetition can be boring, wasteful, and even disrespectful to the reader. A reader can easily go back and read again what you have written; there's no reason to repeat it yourself.

Level of detail

When writing, having a depth of detail while using a complex sentence structure can add a lot of value to your message. Your sentences can be filled with data and be connected with each other to craft a sophisticated message. This detailed style provides a depth and richness to your writing. When speaking, however, the sentence style needs to be simple, while making only one point. Even when people are listening at their best, they can generally only internalize a simple, straightforward message delivered in short sentences.

Now let's dig into writing!

Writing and Reading

So much of our communication today is done through the written word: social media, private messages, texts, and emails. It only stands to reason that you should focus some of your energy on becoming more effective in this form of communication.

To help you improve your writing, here are a few suggestions:

- **Have something to say.** As the writer, it's your responsibility to have a message of value. Your job is to articulate that message in a compelling manner and gain buy-in from the reader. Authenticity, believability, and character are key.

- **Be bold.** If your energy, passion, and enthusiasm are genuine, your message will come across in a stronger way.

- **Admit what you know and what you don't.** Leaders are transparent and able to share that with their readers.

- **Demonstrate confidence.** Muster all of the confidence and capability you can on what you know about the topic, and show that to the reader. Take time to focus on the issue and build to the level of confidence that works for you.

- **Engage your team.** This is one of the most powerful components to build deep credibility, quickly. When writing to a group of people or your team, be interactive and ask open-ended questions that show you really want to hear the answers. Don't be the tactical person whose only interest is to check things off their list. Care about your team, and they will care about what you have to say.

When choosing which method to use when communicating, refer to your Relationship Map and the method the other person likes to use to connect. Whether you use a private message, text, or email should be their choice, not yours. **Be sure to write once and edit twice to craft a clear message.**

Remember to focus on your audience while writing, being empathetic with their circumstances when you attempt to connect through your words. Writing still works today. You simply have to say something they care about.

The Tone of Your Message

When writing, the tone of your message is critical. How does it *sound*? Here are a few categories that your note could fall into. There are no right or wrong ones, but be sure that your message falls into the category you want:

- Soft—This message is meant to be encouraging, empathetic, emotional, and caring. You are conveying a positive message to the recipient.

- Fair—This message is meant to see both sides of an issue or topic. The focus is on being balanced and making sure both sides are heard and conveyed.

- Strong—This message is designed to present a position you have taken that is clear, focused, purposed, and directional. There should be no question as to what you want the reader to take away from reading your note.

- Tough—This message comes from the tough love school. You have something to share that could be hard for the other person to hear, but something you believe needs to be said.

- Stern—This message is for the purpose of correction. The reader has done something you do not want repeated and it is important that you communicate your displeasure with their action and any corrective action you think is appropriate.

You must work not only with the tone of the message, but also with the directness of it. For that, let's introduce the concept of the "velvet hammer." Each time you speak with someone, you must balance the directness of your message (the hammer) with the right amount of empathy and care (the velvet) for the other person. Be too direct without empathy and they will not hear you because they won't think you care about them. Have too much empathy (velvet) and you can lose the clarity and directness of the message, in which case they won't understand what you are trying to communicate.

Remember whom your audience is. When you are broadcasting a note to a large audience, it is likely that there will be a wide range of possible reactions and interpretations. You need to be very careful in your wording to minimize the possible misunderstandings from your message. In most cases, it helps if you strategize what you want to say, how you want it to be received, and to whom the message should be delivered. It's all too common that a leader will write a note designed for just a few and then broadcast it to a large group. The result is that many people feel offended, when what the leader really needed to do was write a private note to a select few. Rule of Thumb: Encourage and recognize in public, and critique and discipline in private. Just like when we talked about making your recognition of accomplishments proportional to the activity and the person, so should you make sure your written communication is proportional to the content and context of your message.

One other consideration to take into account with tone is the personality color of the person with whom you are communicating. From the book *Full Spectrum Success* by Jacob Adamo (2014), we learn to look at the four personality colors and get a basic understanding of what individuals in each color category will need (note: this is a simplistic view of personalities, which is a huge sci in itself):

- Red—They want direct, short communications that allow them to make decisions quickly and find that path to victory.

- Blue—Find a fun, humorous or adventurous way to present your communication. Use stories, gifs, and/or emojis!

- Green—Make sure your communication has lots of data, analysis, conclusions, and a plan of action. Facts, facts, facts.

- Yellow—Make your communication personal, friendly, and genuine. It helps if there is a reference to their family, hobby, vacation, pets, etc.

One comment on the personality colors. Each of us has a strong or dominant color, but we are in fact a combination of all the colors. As a *full palette leader*, we should strive to use our intuition to know which color we should be calling on to be effective. If you are a Red, we still want you to go with your strength, but if the situation calls for Yellow, then bring out the best Yellow you can.

Special Note: Colors are very similar to DISC and both have their roots in Meyers-Briggs Type Indicators. We've chosen the color description primarily for its simplicity and should not be seen as denying the power and usefulness of the other personality evaluations. The Core Values Index (CVI) and Enneagram are also helpful tools in understanding your team and yourself as a leader.

Feeling Connected

Everything we've discussed has focused on actions such as speaking, listening, and writing, but we can't forget about *feeling*. You want each of your communications to be *experienced* and *felt* by the recipient. The goal is not just to gain understanding, but to achieve an emotional response.

When you communicate, you want to be memorable and you want your message to have an impact. There are no rules as to how you do it—writing, speaking, or even video—just find that magic that makes *your* message special. Did your message evoke a memory in the recipient that was profound? Was your message so powerful that a response *had* to happen? Was there a connection so genuine during your communication that people had to take action? Each of us has the ability to make this happen.[4]

How do you know that your connection has reached an emotional level? You listen, you watch, you wait, you ask, and you use your intuition to evaluate all of the signals. When people respond from their emotions, you can tell. Asking a simple question in a Facebook post can be a good test. Review the answers and responses to your post and see what people said. If there are no responses, it's easy to say you weren't effective. The challenge will be to determine *why*. When you do have responses, did those who commented stretch themselves to respond? Were they transparent in their answers? Did anyone learn anything through the post? Did you reach your audience? Answering these questions will help you determine if you had an emotional connection.

Maya Angelou's quote just about says it all—we all want to be remembered for who we are, what we said, and how we impacted others.

> *"I've learned that people will forget what you said, people will forget what you did, but people will never forget how you made them feel."*
>
> –Maya Angelou[*]

How Do I Engage People?

All of this discussion has been about communicating, but what if those on the receiving end of our messages don't respond? Here are some reasons (excuses) people give for not responding and some things you can do to overcome them.

- They are overwhelmed.
  - Reduce the information overload; make it simple for them.
  - Don't get overwhelmed yourself.
- They start off strong in your discussions, then lose interest.
  - Help them get to their why.
  - Get them to stay active.
  - Everyone has a lull; help them recover their momentum.

---

4 David Booth and Masayuki Hachiya (Eds.), The Arts Go to School: Classroom-Based Activities That Focus on Music, Painting, Drama, Movement, Media, and More (Sidebar quotation), Markham, Ontario: Pembroke Publishers (2004, p. 12).

- They miss your handholding. They responded when you were helping them, but when you stopped, they stopped.
  - Time to help them find their independence.
  - Head off their complaining at the start and point them in the direction of their own success.
  - Help them to discover their ownership.
- The business is not their #1 priority.
  - Is their why big enough or important enough for them?
  - Be empathetic to their situation.
- They think the business is going to be easy and that they don't need you.
  - Add value at such at a high level that they can't imagine doing the business without you.
  - Schedule regular calls.
  - Coach them with open-ended questions.

Be persistent, consistent, and present while showing them that you care. Never give up on your team. Don't disappear on them. Be personable and genuine. Close any say/do gaps. You found them and recruited them for a reason; trust yourself and keep on plugging away until you reach them.

Facebook Posts

One of the most common problems we hear about concerning a lack of engagement with people is when you post something on Facebook and no one responds—sigh... Here are a few more tips for when your Facebook post gets little to no response.

- Edit the post—Review your post again. Have another set of eyes also review the post and determine if an edit of the post would help.
- Use a photo to catch their eye – Our world has gone visual for sure. Word only posts too often die on the vine because nothing captured their visual attention.
- Ask for feedback—Contact your inner circle and get their feedback on the post. Perhaps your phrasing was poor or your message was irrelevant?
- Plant a comment—Have one of your friends help you out by commenting on your post. If appropriate, ask them to comment on a specific theme that you point them to.

- Call to action—Is there a call to action in the post? If not, perhaps put one in. Give people something to respond to.

- Delete the post—You missed it. The post really wasn't that good. Don't sweat it; let your frustration go. Delete the post. Better not to have the post cluttering your page.

It's story time!

That is What I *Really* Meant

Iris had been talking to Liz for several weeks now about the compensation plan. This stuff was complicated and really hard to explain, with lots of moving parts. Iris wasn't an expert on this topic and she just wasn't getting through to Liz. Liz had most of the plan down, but couldn't understand the difference between generations and levels. Did she get paid for 3 generations or was that 4 levels down?

Iris thought she'd go through a live example. She prepared a diagram, took out one of her checks, and showed Liz how the generations and levels worked. Liz smiled. Iris thought, "This is it! I've finally gotten through!" Then, Liz spoke:

Liz: Iris, thank you so much for working through that example. It really helped to confirm that I truly don't get this and never will.

Iris: I'm sorry! I thought when you smiled, I had finally explained it well. I really am sorry! I just don't know what to do. I don't know how to explain it any better.

Iris sat there frustrated, sad, and a little mad at herself. These emotions kept washing over her and she was a mess. Then, it dawned on her—this must be what Liz is going through. She feels inadequate or perhaps a little slow because she can't get it. But, it's not her fault, it's mine. I'm not explaining it well. So, she turned to Liz and said:

Iris: Liz, this whole thing is my fault. I should know the plan better. But, can I share with you what that check means to my family and me?

Iris spent the next fifteen minutes telling Liz how her life had been changed by the business. How the money now coming in had changed the lives of her family as well. She put her "why" on the table and showed Liz how to make more money through the bonuses and the strategy she had used.

Liz smiled again, but it was a heartfelt one this time.

Liz: Iris, I don't yet understand the math, but I GET what the bonuses mean now. I feel your confidence in yourself and your team shining through and I hear how this has made a difference in your family. Do you think we could call corporate to get the math down together?

Iris: Liz, it would be my pleasure.

Discussion

Why didn't Liz get the message the first time? What could Iris have done earlier? What made the difference when Iris changed her approach? Why did sharing about her family impact Liz?

How are you going to communicate your next message?

The Path Forward

In this module, we covered how connection is the driving force of communication. If we don't connect, communication only transfers information.

We reviewed the reason listening is so important, even more so than speaking. However, when you do speak, then being yourself, knowing your audience, and engaging them on an emotional level can make all the difference.

We also looked at our writing, including what we need to do to stand out from all of the other messages a person receives.

Lastly, we discovered what it means to affect someone's feelings and how that will make you and your message memorable.

Action Required

In preparation for our next group meeting, please complete the exercise on the next page.

Discussion Framework

Use this page to capture your preliminary thoughts about this module's content. Each quadrant has questions that are provided to help stimulate your thoughts and reflections. This is not a quiz and there are no wrong answers. It is an opportunity for deep self-awareness, so capture whatever seems appropriate to you.

	INTERNAL	EXTERNAL
INDIVIDUAL	**REFLECT** What did you read about this week that caught your eye and caused you to reflect? Id like a "soft" Id like to have a softer message I have strong messages pg 50 emoji gif whats new good in your life	**ADOPT** What would you like to adopt as a going forward behavior or process that you picked up from this week's module? Improve my Listening skills
GROUP	**INQUIRE** What question would you like to ask the group concerning the topic(s) in the module? business is not my builders #1 priority. How to figure out why?	**SHARE** What insight, principle, or leadership precept did you want to share with the group?

COACHING

In Downline Leadership, **we define Coaching as being a catalyst for the growth and development of others**. When you engage as a coach, you can shape the development of others, empowering them to act both independently and in concert with their team. When you invest in others by coaching, they become invaluable, productive, and impactful. By doing this, you gain leverage in your business from having improved downline performance *through* your extended team.

To function in the role of coach, your mindset must shift to one of inquiry, curiosity, increasing self-awareness, and empowerment. Coaches are looking to the future. As they invest in people, they are not only looking for a return from the current team, but from the extended downline as well. When your team invests in the people around them, those people grow and increasingly contribute to the business as well as the business of others. This investment can pay large dividends in the future not only for you, but also for the one's you coach.

Module Overview

As a result of experiencing this module, you will:

- Examine the foundational elements of coaching (what it is, why it works, why you do it, and how it applies).
- Contrast Group Coaching with 1:1 Coaching.
- Determine when to Coach, as well as when it's appropriate to Direct, Teach, or Mentor.
- Explore the heart of coaching, how the leader develops people, and why it's important.

What is Coaching?

Coaching is the action of bringing out new ideas, insights, and answers from the other person. Coaching is all about *pulling from* the person and not *pushing into* the person. Coaches try to help others have greater self-awareness and realize personal growth. This also means that a coach may challenge the other person to be that *best* version of themselves. There will be times that the coach will have to use tough love to show the person that they care enough about them to ask the hard questions.

It is important to note here that there are two types of coaching: Group Coaching and 1:1 Coaching. We will expand on the differences between the two types of coaching later in this module.

Coaching Process

Coaches use active listening, feedback loops, empowerment, and penetrating, open-ended questions to help other people develop. As the people being coached realize their capabilities, they achieve more and impact others.

> *"I never cease to be amazed at the power of the coaching process to draw out the skills or talent that was previously hidden within an individual, and which invariably finds a way to solve a problem previously thought unsolvable."*
> **–John Russell, Managing Director, Harley-Davidson Europe Ltd.**
>
> *In Coaching to Success by Neil Nutburn (2011)*

Asking questions

Asking open-ended questions is at the core of coaching. These questions are thought provoking and focused on what the person wants to create or do in the future. If you do ask a question that looks into the past, it's to help them reflect and interpret the previous events for the purpose of putting a future action plan together. Coaches help people look at possible actions, resources, and information, and provide the support they need to create the solution they are trying to obtain.

Building a strong relationship with the people on your team enables you to ask these coaching questions. Many times, these questions are not easy to answer, as the person has to reflect and dig deep to respond. At times the questions can challenge the individual's previous thinking, causing him or her to have a mindset shift. The coaching process requires a relationship built on mutual trust—not just with the person, but also with the group (if you're doing group coaching). It's a safe and trusting environment within the group that enables the group coaching approach to thrive.

When team members are able to solve more problems on their own, they will remember the coaching sessions; this will further build your credibility with them. They will also know that you care about them and are truly interested in helping them grow.

Learning NOT to ask the wrong questions

Inappropriate coaching questions can stifle the coaching experience for the other person. There are two common types of questions that should be avoided. First, don't use closed-ended questions, where the only answer is yes or no. These types of questions rarely reveal any special insight or idea, as they merely confirm or deny your assumptions. These questions restrict the thinking process as the participant can *only* answer yes or no. These closed-ended questions can also be perceived as embarrassing, condescending, or humiliating.

Second, don't try to solve the problem for them by asking a solutioning question. This is one of the hardest things for a coach to avoid, as we tend to want to solve problems. We want to be the mentor and have all the answers. When you ask a "solutioning" type of question, you are guiding the person along a path that *you* think is the right one to take. Instead, remember this is not about *you*, it's about helping *them* solve *their* own problems, with *their* solutions, not *yours*. If you plant the wrong seeds, you may inhibit creativity and innovation, robbing them of the opportunity to figure out the answer themselves, or not allow them to fail and learn. This is why curiosity and inquiry-based questions are key. They assist in promoting their own answers to their own challenges.

For example, we usually teach our children how to tie their shoes the same way we learned, hence the concept has developed that there is only one way to tie your shoe. However, when you go to a running store, you find out that there are actually dozens of ways to tie your shoes, depending on what problem with your feet you are trying to solve. Therefore, it makes sense to ask people what challenge they are facing and how *they* would like to solve it, before you step in and solve it for them. **People are more likely to take corrective action and change their behaviors when they feel ownership for the solution.** If you've influenced them toward *your* solution, they have less ownership of it.

Listening

Listening is a critical element of coaching and communication. When you are being a coach, your listening needs to step up a level. It is no longer about acquiring data. As you listen, you have to hear the meanings behind the words and sometimes even see the message in the person's body language.

A big shift in the coaching mindset is moving from **listening to respond** to **listening to understand**. Here are a few tips on listening as it relates to being a coach.

- Be present, be there, be available, and be ready!

- Listen with your intuition. What does your gut say they are saying or not saying? How do *you* feel about the discussion? What does your intuition say about how *they* feel?

- Listen carefully to their answers. The very best questions coaches ask are not the first question, but the fifth question in a series of questions and answers as they dig deeper.

  o How do you get to the fifth question?

    ▪ Be curious. This especially helps with the first four questions.

    ▪ Listen carefully to each answer and think carefully before you ask the next question.

    ▪ Practice patience, and don't be afraid of silence.

    ▪ Be creative. Let your intuition guide you into areas that may seem off the beaten path, but frequently result in new ideas for the other person to reflect on.

- Be sensitive to how the other person is answering. What is their overall demeanor? Are they threatened by the questions? Are they embarrassed to answer? Are they being too introverted? Are they calm?

- Listen for the smallest of details, and be open to changing directions at any time. Frequently it is the off-hand comment by the participant that, when heard and acted on with an open-ended question, yields the most surprising and valuable dialogue.

- When you think the other person has more to share, instead of asking another question, sometimes you can simply say, "Tell me more." This small statement can open up a floodgate of information, trust, and insight.

Feedback Loops

During coaching, the person or team might determine there is something they want to work on and improve. One of the ways for them to evaluate their progress is to set up feedback loops.

Thomas Goetz, author of *The Decision Tree*, describes feedback loops as follows:

> The premise of a feedback loop is simple: Provide people with information about their actions in real time, then give them a chance to change those actions, pushing them toward better behaviors.[5]

Feedback example—You believe that you are spending too much time explaining things during your 101 class. Instead of being direct and brief, then asking for questions, you tend to have long, drawn-out explanations. But, the crowd "seems" to enjoy your rambles. To get more clarity, you set up a feedback loop with Jane before your next class. You ask Jane to specifically look for long speeches and to record the situation that got you there. The feedback from Jane will help you to better understand the circumstances when you ramble and why.

You can help someone set up a feedback loop to facilitate the flow of information back to them for evaluation, reflection, and use. The goal is to narrow the gap between their current behavior and the desired behavior.

As they stay open to feedback, real change can occur. They can make adjustments in real time and implement new strategies to move forward.

The important thing is for the person to be intentional and specific about what they want feedback on. This makes the feedback loop much more than getting an opinion. You, in the role of coach, can help introduce the idea and then encourage and support others in their use of it.

Here is a quick summary of what a feedback loop looks like:

1. Determine what you specifically want feedback on.

2. Talk with someone whom you trust to provide the feedback BEFORE you do anything.

---

5   Thomas Goetz, *Wired Magazine*, June 19, 2011

3. You take an action.

4. The action has one or more effects.

5. The important effects of this action are presented back to you by the person you had talked with earlier.

6. This loop is repeated regularly.

Factors to keep in mind when setting up a feedback loop are the following:

1. Speed—How fast is the feedback received?

2. Measurability—Is the feedback in a format that can be measured and analyzed?

3. Context—Is the feedback collected (or received) relevant to the issue?

4. Motivation—Is the feedback impacted or influenced by the motivations of the person giving the feedback?

5. Trust—Do you trust the person giving you the feedback?

Empowerment and Failing Forward

When you believe that the other person has the solution within them, you have to allow them to discover and implement that solution. That means you have to let them go with their idea and embrace their newfound empowerment.

> *"Fail early, fail often, but always fail forward."*
> –John C. Maxwell
>
> In Thomas Nelson, Failing Forward, Nashvillle, TN (2000, p. 114).

Occasionally, that may mean letting them fail. If this happens, the power is in having the person/team learn for themselves what worked for them and what didn't. This path of discovering their own idea or solution, executing it, failing, reflecting, and trying again encourages true learning.

The Leverage Factor

Leaders want to achieve success with every team they lead, and coaching plays an important part in that success. To achieve success, it helps to have the best performers, or at least performers who are at their best. The reality is you don't deliver results with the people you **wished** you had; you deliver results with the people you **do** have. Simply put—you must lead the ones you have, and it helps considerably if you have honed your coaching skills to bring out their best. This absolutely applies to your business, where everyone in your downline owns his or her own business. You can't always pick who is on your team (or theirs), so **lead the ones you're with,** and lead them where you know to go!

Coaching helps your team improve their skills, capabilities, and talents. This raised level of performance creates leverage in a few ways. It reduces their dependency on you by increasing their self-dependence. This increases engagement and performance levels overall.

Furthermore, when people perform better, they can take on more responsibility and ownership for their portion of the overall downline. They spend less time asking you questions and solve more problems on their own.

Heart of Coaching

The heart of leadership is caring about people. *The heart of coaching is caring about their growth and development.* When you care about people and how they are growing and learning, then you are acting as coach. Caring about the people on your team means that you want to help them, develop them, challenge them, encourage them, and empower them. Your focus is on the people, who they are and who they want to be. One of the ways to do that is to "lean into their agenda." Focus not only on what they care about, but also on how they are going to get it done. When you do that well, they move to the next level and you get a side benefit of improved performance on your team.

In an ideal world where everything worked perfectly, there likely wouldn't be a need for coaching. In the real world, there are almost always opportunities for improvement—either overcoming challenges or producing results better and faster. The best way to tap into the natural strengths and talents of the people around you is by adopting the coaching role.

When you spend time with people, coaching them, they see that you respect their talent and intellect. They learn that you care about them and their decisions. When you have established that caring foundation, you have entered into the heart of coaching.

Lastly, it is frequently important to ask *permission* to coach. You want to ensure that the other person is comfortable being asked open-ended question after question. This is not a requirement, but use your intuition to make sure that you've set the right environment for the coaching session.

Coaching is a profession

Before we go any further, we want to clarify that your role as a coach should be kept to business-specific topics and issues. Coaching is a dedicated, full-time profession that requires a wide range of high-end skills and competencies. You haven't been trained or equipped to fill that professional role for others, nor is that the primary function of your role as Leader.

Instead of becoming that full-time professional coach, we want you to recognize the power and benefits of applying a limited set of coaching skills at key moments with your team to achieve higher levels of success.

When engaging in a coaching dialogue, it's important to understand the boundaries of the conversation. If you focus on the future needs of the person as it relates to a business outcome, you're on safe ground. Coaches look forward with a purpose of growth. Lastly, be mindful that coaching is neither therapy nor counseling; you're not a psychiatrist nor psychologist.

Let's share some common pitfalls Coaches fall into.

The Most Common Mistakes New Coaches Make

Practicing the *mechanics* of coaching without having made the deep personal shifts in attitudes, beliefs, and assumptions *toward being a* coach is perhaps the largest mistake a coach can make. This shift to caring about other people and desiring to bring out their best through coaching must be evident and real. If they don't know you have the heart of a coach, then just asking a random open-ended question won't make you their coach. Here are a few other mistakes coaches make:

- Misunderstanding the principle of coachability:
  - Not every moment is a coachable moment.
  - Not every topic is a coachable topic for every person.
  - Not every person is coachable.
- Overestimating the short-term results from coaching.
- Failing to build strong relationships that create a trusting space for coaching to occur.
- Trying to use coaching to *fix* other people.

- Saying "always" and "never" when talking to the other person. Rarely are either true.

- Being a "Re-stater"—where you restate your question, over and over again. Sometimes this is due to second-guessing yourself, or because you are trying to perfect the question.

- Being a "Machine Gunner"—where you ask a dozen questions, one after another, without giving the person a chance to answer.

- Being a "Multiple Choicer"—where you ask an open-ended question, then give multiple options for answers (these are *your* choices, not *theirs*).

The Coaching Process in Action

Perhaps the best way to understand the Coaching Process is to see the process in action.

Below is an example of Erin coaching Melissa after noticing the constant use of discounts in Melissa's Facebook posts. Look carefully at the situation and get a feeling for what Melissa is going through. Then review Erin's probing questions. See how she was able to help Melissa work through some of her issues, come to a decision on her own, and develop a new plan.

Background: For the last three months, Melissa has been sending out post after post providing discounts off the oils listed at retail pricing in order to get people interested in the oils. Erin is Melissa's upline and hasn't understood Melissa's strategy.

Erin: Hey Melissa! How are you doing? I just saw your latest post on DiGize essential oil and your offer of 24% off. Would it be OK if I asked you a few questions?

Melissa: Sure, Erin.

Erin: I was wondering about your strategy. Why are you giving people the retail price, then offering all of these discounts?

Melissa: Well, it's pretty simple. I live in an area where people won't buy anything unless there's a discount or special sale price on it.

Erin: How's that working for you?

Melissa: To be honest, it hasn't worked out as well as I'd hoped.

Erin: I'm sorry to hear that. Why do you think it isn't working?

Melissa: It seems that unless I put a discount on every oil, no one will buy any oils at all. They keep waiting for my latest special of the week, and not buying any of the other oils that I don't have listed with a discount.

Erin: Sounds like me when I go to the store. What do you think would happen if you focused on the oils themselves instead of just the price?

Melissa: That's easy. I'd lose all my sales for sure!

Erin: (chuckle) I love your passion, Melissa! What are some other successful business people in your downline doing?

Melissa: A couple of them are doing what I'm doing.

Erin: What type of results have they achieved?

Melissa: (sigh) Pretty much the same as me.

Erin: What about the other successful ones? What other ways, besides highlighting price, do others get people interested in the oils in their market?

Melissa: Jeanie seems to share oil stories and testimonials.

Erin: How is she doing with that?

Melissa: She seems to move a lot more kits than I do, but not nearly as many single oils like my discounts do.

Erin: What does that say to you?

Melissa: Well...Jeanie's customers seem to end up with a broader interest in the oils, and she makes more commission by selling kits than on single oils.

Erin: Hmmm... Tell me more.

Melissa: It may lead to a deeper love of the oils if they try more oils and not just the ones on sale. My commission would probably increase, too. Maybe I could try a few posts that focus on my oil stories.

Erin: Why would you want to change your approach?

Melissa: I've got to do something different or I'm going to keep on getting the same results.

Erin: Sounds like you've got an idea on what to do next and a reason behind the strategy. What's next?

Did you also see all of the open-ended questions from Erin and how one-on-one coaching can really help people? Now, let's move on to discuss group coaching.

Group Coaching versus 1:1 Coaching

While most of the fundamentals of coaching work for both group coaching and 1:1 coaching, there are some differences.

Because there are other people present during group coaching, you need to be sensitive to the overall environment and engagement level of the group. You can't just launch into open-ended questions with a person, singling them out, without setting the stage. If a group coaching situation presents itself, here are few tips to consider.

- Gauge the emotional state of the person in the group to see if they would benefit from coaching.

- Assess if they can withstand the pressure of having others around during the coaching moment.

- Ask them directly if they would be OK with being asked some questions.

- Involve the other team members where appropriate, even allowing them to ask questions as well. This can easily become an Intentional Story exercise and an extension of the group coaching session. However, you must carefully facilitate the session to ensure the integrity of the group and that the person with the opportunity never feels threatened.

- Ensure the questions are truly helping the person solve their own problem and are not the group telling the person what to do or leading him or her down some other path.

- Control the pace of the discussion, making sure you are matching the tone and pace of the person so they are comfortable participating.

- Constantly measure the room and the participant. Are you adding value?

- At the end, ask the participant what his or her reflection on the experience was, if they felt comfortable sharing what they learned, and what action they are going to take.

- Coaching is focused on the person; facilitation is focused on the meeting flow and overall group discussion. They're different, and you'll do both in a group setting.

The opportunities to coach are quite common if you are open to them and not stuck in other roles. What other roles, you ask?

Coach First and Role Agility

In addition to the role of the coach, there are other leadership roles in the form of Director, Teacher, and Mentor. The principle in play here is *situational leadership*, wherein leaders adopt a particular role based on their situation. Let's describe these roles, and also relook at the Coach role and why taking a coach-first approach is so important.

Director (you tell others)

This role deals with *tasks, transactions, or tactical matters*. The Director role is valuable when *communicating guidelines or prescribing a course of action*, especially during a crisis, when time is short, or when efficiency is key and there is only a small window for the communication to take place.

There is very little interaction when you are in this role. The primary force is a *push* from you to them. If there is a fire in the building and safety is paramount, you want to be in Director mode. Overusing or misusing this mode, however, has a significant downside. Since it's the least relational mode, it doesn't drive engagement or interaction, nor does it favorably demonstrate your capabilities as a leader. Using the Director role at the wrong time can drive your team further from you, not closer.

Teacher (you show others)

In this role, you are passing along skills and knowledge, usually in a deliberate manner. When you have determined from the answers to your coaching questions (see coach-first approach below) that there is a gap in understanding, it's time to teach. You either teach the participant(s) yourself or bring in a subject matter expert to share the appropriate methods and/or information. In some ways, it's similar to the Director role, but it includes more context about *why* a particular course of action is being taken.

During this dialogue, interaction is higher than when in Director mode, yet the primary force is still a push in the direction of you to them. The best way to use the Teacher mode is to make it relational and engaging, while still protecting your time constraints and other requirements. Remember the good teachers you've had and emulate how they interacted with you.

Mentor (you share with others)

When in the Mentor role, you pass along your experience and wisdom based on your journey and your reflections. This usually happens when the other person has invited you to share your thoughts in the hopes they may learn from your experience. They really want to know what you would do if you were in their situation. This can be a very powerful role and impact others greatly, but you must be careful that the other person does not copy your exact steps, as each person's situation will be unique to them. It's the responsibility of the Mentor to ensure that they only say what they would do in their situation while the other person listens, learns, and determines what they will apply (if anything) to their *own* circumstance.

The Mentor role can be very relational, last a long time, and have a huge impact on others. Leaders are in this role often.

Coach (you ask others)

This role is the highest manifestation of empowerment and engagement when relating to others.

Accordingly, it is extremely challenging and requires the highest level of time and commitment. In many ways, it is the opposite of the other three roles. It doesn't matter what you know, what you did or would do, or what you'd like to say—the only thing that matters is the other person. Your role is to ask insightful open-ended questions that help that person discover their own truth and their own solution to their problem. What an opportunity for leadership!

One of the other benefits of coaching is the opportunity to focus on the other person's strength. Way too much time is spent on people's shortcomings and weaknesses. Instead, a Coach will find a great amount of success by pulling the strengths from the other person and helping that person to identify, acknowledge, and grow those strengths. When people are operating in the area or zone of their strength, they achieve more—it's that simple.

The Coach role is the one where your primary purpose is to help develop another person, maybe even another leader. The order is different from the other roles that all started with *you*. Coaching starts with *others*.

Coach First, then Pivot

We also want to highly suggest you adopt the mentality of *Coach First* before implementing the other leadership roles. Using a Coach-First approach means that you seek first to understand. This is accomplished by asking open-ended questions and avoiding making any assumptions. You show respect to your teammates by trying to find out what the issue or challenge is and if you can help. It's difficult to gain this information without adopting the coach-first approach.

Another benefit of using the coach-first approach is that it helps leaders avoid *duplicating* themselves. As leaders, we don't want copies of ourselves: We want unique, empowered leaders acting out of their own area of strength. By coaching and specifically using the coach-first approach, we hope to *replicate* ourselves. In this instance, replication means that the other person will take from you what they see as fitting well with them. Using your influence, you are able to plant a leadership seed in the other person, not for the purpose of copying behavior or action, but to help them create leadership within themselves. While duplication means to clone or copy yourself at the tactical level, replication means to empower others to take your strategic leadership principles and develop their own vision of leadership. The coach-first approach helps to achieve this, while the other three roles tend to foster duplication.

That doesn't mean there isn't a place for the other three roles of leadership; rather, it's the job of the leader to determine the right role for the situation. By taking a coach-first approach, you now have information to guide you in determining which role to choose. After you have asked questions and heard what has been going on, you will then be empowered to choose between the appropriate roles, and can fluidly pivot and 'switch hats' transitioning to teacher or mentor roles as needed. We like to think of it like the old four-color pens. All four are part of one pen, and you simply click to change the color of the ink. Similar to the pen, you have the flexibility and fluidity of multiple roles, and starting with the "coach first" as default will help you to know which role is most needed. Now... It's story time!

One more change!

Anita, Stephanie, Robin, and Jennifer were having their weekly team meeting and Stephanie was beside herself. "One more change from Corporate and I'm going to explode. Did you see that we now only have twenty days to move someone when they enroll?"

The group jumped in and everyone started to complain either about this change or another one that had been made. Then, someone commented on a change that actually hadn't even occurred, and that's when Robin reigned everyone in.

"OK, let's talk for a minute about these changes and see if we can't help each other out. Stephanie, you mentioned the twenty-day change limit. Why is that change frustrating to you?"

Stephanie thought for a minute, "Well, I really liked the thirty days we used to have. I could wait until the end of the month to see where the person needed to be placed for helping others in my downline reach their goals. Who was popping up business? Who needed a kick start? Which leg did I need to build more? I could put them wherever in the earlier ranks, but

as the ranks went higher, it made a difference and I needed to wait longer. Did I need to put it in my leg 2 or in my PGV leg 3? Which needed it more? It gave me more time to make sure I was putting someone in the right leg."

Anita jumped in, "Yes, but is there really a benefit to the extra ten days? I feel like I have my best idea on where to place someone in the first five days; after that I'm just guessing. What do you think, Jennifer?"

Jennifer had been thinking to herself and had been quiet, "I actually prefer the twenty-day limit. I make the best decision I can and then it gets off my plate. I don't miss the extra ten days. Honestly? I tended to waste them. Stephanie, what did you use the extra ten days for?"

Stephanie said, "I'm so busy I really needed those last few days to make a decision. But when Anita was speaking, it made me think that I was just procrastinating and waiting until the last few days before the time was up. Wow, I never thought about it that way. I just thought Corporate was messing with us again."

Robin added "Stephanie, we can all feel that way sometimes, but what happens when we let that feeling take over?"

Anita answered, "Then we play the victim and we're no longer responsible for our businesses—it's all Corporate's fault. But Robin, Corporate isn't perfect. Sometimes they really do screw up. What are we to do then?"

Before Robin could answer, Anita piped in, "Then we get together, discuss the pros and cons of the change, and make sure we can give Corporate solid examples of why their new policy doesn't make sense. When this group gets together, we're just better than what we would be alone. Robin, thank you for making this group better!"

Robin replied, "Anita, thank you for that compliment, but I want everyone to know that it's all of us working together, asking each other the tough questions, that brings out the best from us. We're definitely a force to be reckoned with, don't you think?"

At that, everyone nodded their heads up and down. "What a great meeting," they thought. "Just when it looked like a pity party, we pulled together and started getting real."

Discussion:

What do you think of Robin's coaching of the group? What would you have done differently? What would have happened if Robin hadn't stepped in? How would you have responded to Corporate on the change in days if you had the chance?

What did you think about Jennifer being quiet? Why should you be quiet? Here are a few possible reasons:

- Remaining quiet shows respect to the other person.
- It allows time for your intuition to get in gear.

- It allows you to be reflective.

- You focus on their agenda, not yours.

- It allows the other person to think of his or her own answer.

The Path Forward

In this module, we explored how a coach pulls from their teammates and how that helps them increase their self-awareness to become the best version of themselves.

We also looked at what it means to ask open-ended and probing questions, both in a one-on-one, as well as a group setting.

We reviewed the benefits of using a coach-first approach to engage with the team, as well as how a leader adjusts his or her role based upon the situation. We dug into the heart of coaching and why it matters to genuinely care about the people on your team.

We will be discussing these concepts in more detail during the group session.

Action Required

In preparation for our next group meeting, please complete the exercise on the next page.

Discussion Framework

Use this page to capture your preliminary thoughts about this module's content. Each quadrant has questions that are provided to help stimulate your thoughts and reflection. This is not a quiz and there are no wrong answers. It is an opportunity to deepen self-awareness, so capture whatever seems appropriate to you.

	INTERNAL	EXTERNAL
INDIVIDUAL	**Reflect** What did you read about this week that caught your eye and caused you to reflect?	**Adopt** What would you like to adopt as a going-forward behavior or process that you picked up from this week's module?
GROUP	**Inquire** What question would you like to ask the group concerning the topic(s) in the module?	**Share** What insight, principle, or leadership precept did you want to share with the group?

Be sure to see the next page for the Appendix of this chapter.

Appendix

The coaching process is an iterative one, requiring careful listening and thoughtful questions. As you go through each iteration with another person, different questions may come to mind based on what you hear and where the other person wants to go. Accordingly, Coaching is NOT asking a bunch of questions off a sheet of paper.

That being said, at times it helps to have suggestions for when you're stuck. In these instances, you may find the questions below helpful to get you going again. The questions come from the book *Co-Active Coaching.*[6*] Add these to your favorite ones, like "What would it look like?" and "Tell me more?"

Assessment/Clarification/Elaboration

- How do you feel about it?
- What is your assessment of the situation?
- What is the part that is not yet clear?
- What concerns you the most about it?
- What else is happening?

Evaluation/Example

- What is the opportunity here? What is the challenge?
- How does this fit with your plans?
- What is an example?
- What have you done in the past?

Exploration/Learning/Inquiry

- What do you want to explore further?
- What are your other options?
- What would you do differently in the future?

---

6   Sandahl and Whitworth, *Co-Active Coaching,* Boston and London: Kimsey-House, Nicholas Brealey Publishing (2011).

- What did you learn from this?
- What could you have done to handle the situation better?
- What led up to it?

Implementation/Integration/Outcomes

- What will you do?
- What will you take away from this?
- How can you make sure you remember what you have learned?
- How would you pull all this together?
- What is your desired outcome?
- What do you want?
- How will you know you have achieved it?

Planning

- What do you plan to do about it?
- What kind of plan do you need to create?
- What could you do to improve the situation?

Substance

- What seems to be the main obstacle?
- What seems to be the trouble?
- What is stopping you from moving forward?

OWNERSHIP AND ACCOUNTABILITY

Having ownership is when you lay claim to something as being completely yours. You are not a steward, nor are you a caretaker. Instead, you are the owner, and everything that happens is your responsibility. In the Downline Leadership world, you go from being a person who manages his or her own orders and helps a few people here and there, to a person who owns one's entire business. You own your customers, your team, your downline, and your corporate relations. Ownership happens when you make a powerful, internal choice that no one else can impose upon you. It happens when you care. It comes with higher risks *and* higher rewards. And did you notice we said it was a choice? You have to make a conscious and purposeful decision to take ownership of your business, team, and downline. Ownership can't be given to you, delegated to you, or dropped on you. **You choose to own your business— it doesn't happen any other way.** Having an ownership attitude and creating a sense of ownership in those around you is the responsibility of a leader.

One more attribute of ownership of a network marketing business is the concept of co-ownership. As an owner, you have the opportunity to see your downline as co-owners. When this happens, ownership takes on a whole new meaning. Truly we are all in this together! As one owner grows, other co-owners grow.

Module Overview

In exploring this module, you will

- Explore the nature of ownership and why it's important to have it.

- Determine the differences and intersections between ownership and accountability.

- Recognize what it takes to create a sense of ownership for yourself and others.

- Understand how having a sense of ownership for your business increases the likelihood of success.

A word of caution: it's easy to read this chapter and think over and over again: "I DO take ownership of my business. What I need is to figure out how to help my team own THEIR business!" After all, if you are reading this book (and even more so, if you are participating in a Downline Leadership coaching group), you have 'skin in the game' and are committed to increasing your leadership skills. You already have proven leadership success to achieve your rank, and it can be frustrating to feel as though you are the only 'leader' on your team.

Avoid the temptation to just blame your team for a lack of ownership, and get really honest. Ask yourself good open-ended questions while reading this chapter. Questions like: What level of ownership do I really have? What have I owned too much of? Where have I enabled or disabled my team rather than empowering them? What part of this responsibility/ownership issue did I cause, and how can I address that? Also pay careful attention to the bullet-pointed lists later in this chapter, since they will give you tangible action steps to take to turn around the accountability & ownership culture of your team.

What is Ownership?

Ownership screams out "I've got it!" It requires commitment, trust, and a willingness to be involved with something *greater than your own individual needs*. Ownership requires courage, risk, command, compassion, influence, drive, and persistence. When you take ownership of your business and then bring the results home with your team and customers, it can be a deeply rewarding and enriching experience for all—especially you!

A leader who demonstrates ownership has an emotional investment in his or her business, team, and downline. This is someone who has discovered meaning and importance in the people who constitute their team. Additionally, this leader is always thinking about how to help the team achieve their goals as well as his or her individual goals. Quite simply, the leader exhibits ownership of a business when he or she embraces all of the people in that business and all of its responsibilities. No matter what happens in your business, *you* are responsible for it. From corporate missing a shipment, to a member of your team making a mistake on their order, to a customer backing out of an order on the last day of the month—you own it!

Ownership does not mean you have to be the subject matter expert (SME) on every product or every process; it simply means you have to be the one who chooses to take full responsibility. Knowledge is needed, but not SME levels of expertise in every aspect of the business. Ownership stands outside of specific areas of knowledge about the business and takes the big picture view. The WHOLE business needs to achieve results, and the owner takes the responsibility to hold his or her team accountable to complete their tasks. This includes the challenges within the business that are frequently seen as "someone else's problem."

Any team member can show ownership of a transaction or activity. They do that by linking the activity to the bigger picture of success for the business and satisfaction for the customer. When they go that extra mile and they are doing it with a greater purpose in mind, then they are acting like owners. Think for a moment… Whom do you know who exemplifies ownership? What are some of the ways they do it? How are they consistent about their resolve to deliver success no matter what they face?

Time to explore the difference between ownership and accountability.

Ownership versus Accountability

Accountability is making sure *something* gets done. Ownership is having the responsibility to make sure *everything* gets done. Ownership represents the deepest level of emotional commitment and responsibility to the business. Ownership links to your passion to deliver results and solutions. Accountability is external and easily measured. Ownership is internal, intangible, and connects back to a single moment in time when a leader inwardly says, "This business is mine." Ownership is recognized in a leader who goes above and beyond his or her strict accountability to the business and customer. Accountability tends to be a subset or a piece of ownership.

Accountability is foundational and objective. It is at the task or activity level. It is about those things that can be counted or measured and that are easy to connect with the needs of the business. It can be focused inward as you hold yourself accountable, or outward as you hold others accountable or they hold you accountable. Ownership is about those things you can't measure, things that can be subjective, or that are at the strategic or customer level. Behaviors like commitment, full engagement, utilizing experience, and good judgment exhibit a sense of ownership.

An owner strives to do the right thing and doesn't use a list of tasks (accountability level items) as an excuse for doing the wrong thing. While accountability is important, it's your sense of ownership that drives you to look behind the list of actions to be taken, getting at *why* the tasks need to happen, and how the tasks lead to increased success. Accountability takes you only so far; ownership takes you the rest of the way.

An owner recognizes that having the numbers *look* good in the middle is less important than having the numbers *be* good at the end. A leader committed to ownership understands that all the spit and polish along the way is for naught if success cannot be reached or if customers aren't happy.

When a person acts solely from an accountability perspective, there is always the temptation to avoid unpleasant situations or to cast blame. If you can convince somebody it's not your job, then it can't possibly be your fault. However, that's not ownership. Someone who takes ownership of an activity knows that there is no shifting of responsibility. There is one place that the buck stops—with them.

Let's dig into Accountability before returning to ownership:

Accountability

Accountability is one of the key components of Downline Leadership. It's very difficult to deliver success if you're unable to hold yourself and others accountable.

Accountability is more than just being responsible for getting something done. It begins before you've committed to do something, continues through the "get it done" phase, and ends with reviewing the results. It requires that people connect with their definition of success, understand how to get to it, and put their integrity on the line to achieve their success. You need to be able to support your teammates in going through the same discovery.

To reach the next level of effectiveness, leaders create a supporting culture, an *Accountability Culture*. An Accountability Culture exists when everyone holds themselves accountable to their success. Success can be defined on a task, project, or business level. Raising the level of self-accountability is what leaders do!

Creating an Accountability Culture

You Hold Yourself Accountable

Creating an Accountability Culture starts with you. The expectations you have of yourself should be higher than what others expect of you. While this may seem implicit, you as the leader need to make it explicit and visible to others. Without this first step, an Accountability Culture cannot be adequately created. If you're not willing to hold yourself accountable, then why should you expect others to be held accountable?

You can choose to evidence accountability in any number of ways. You could make a point of showing up on time for meetings and calls, along with making a public declaration that you are committing to do that. You might announce that you'll return all private messages within 4 hours. These are simply two examples of any number of ways personal accountability can be implemented.

Holding yourself accountable means taking responsibility, keeping your promises, and honoring your commitments. Every time you hold yourself accountable and follow through, your Leadership Engine revs faster and more effectively.

Start the dialogue with questions. Remember that each team member owns his or her own business. Your first priority is to support them, but part of that support is helping everyone on the team to have a higher level of accountability to themselves and others. Here are some questions to get the accountability conversation with a team member flowing:

- What kind of accountability is most motivating and helpful for you?
- Do you want me/others to hold you accountable? If so, how?
- What level of flexibility does everyone need to succeed?
- How do you want to share improvement ideas?

Continue the dialogue with values you and the team hold dear. Express the ones you believe in and encourage the group to discuss them further. Here are some to consider:

- We are responsible for our decisions.

- No denials or excuses.

- No blaming others or our circumstances.

- We have shared success and shared failure, so we are accountable to each other.

- We are committed to improve.

Engage the team in dialogue along the way.

- What's going well?

- What isn't going well?

- How are you going to achieve your planned level of success?

- What changes do you need to make to get there? How will you hold ourselves accountable for these new changes? When will you make the changes, and how will you measure the results?

Allow the dialogue to evolve over time. You don't create an Accountability Culture in one meeting. Over time, you can have various accountability checks to see how others perceive the culture. With your team, you could even hold your own mastermind group to discuss accountability! With an effective culture in place, you ensure that each person in the team is holding themselves accountable for the right reasons.

You'll appreciate it when you've fostered this environment with your team. It will free up your time and bandwidth to focus on higher-value activities, because you know your teammates are holding themselves accountable to do what they said they would do!

The Four Tendencies

Gretchen Rubin's study of "The Four Tendencies"[7] explains why some people thrive in a high accountability culture and why others resist. Understanding the basic framework of the question, 'How do people respond to expectations?'

---

7   *The Four Tendencies*, by Gretchen Rubin, 2017, Harmony Books, NY, NY

can transform a team's ownership and accountability culture and dramatically reduce frustration, rebellion, say-do gaps, and disengagement.

Important note: While it is tempting to try to correlate these tendencies with the personality colors we discussed earlier, these are not at all analogous. We recommend taking her online quiz, reading the book, and watching her videos, but here is a short description of the 4 different accountability/motivation tendencies.

The 4 Tendencies Framework holds practical answers if you've ever wondered:

- Why can I keep my word to others, but not to myself?

- Why do I resist good advice from my upline and seek the opinions of other experts in my company?

- How do I work with someone who actively refuses to do what I suggest – or does the opposite?

- How do I stop my leaders from quitting the business?

- How can I convince my team to do their IPAs (income producing activities) and EOM (end of month) hustle?

- And, the biggest challenge sometimes – How do I get myself to do what I want? Why do I resist doing the things I know I need to do?

Understanding the Four Tendencies makes this all much easier.

- The Upholder
- The Obliger
- The Questionier
- The Rebel

The Upholder responds well to outer and inner expectations. If they are asked to do something, or make up their mind to do it, they will. They keep their word and feel good about it. Upholders are the easiest to work with and do well in a culture of accountability; all you need to do is get their commitment, and it's as good as done.

Obligers keep their word to others, but can let themselves down easily. Obligers do very well with accountability partners, checklists, and appreciate phone call & text reminders. To help a stalled obliger, help them be more accountable to a team or to you on public items or team projects, and they will shine. Putting a class on the schedule for an obliger or an upholder means IT WILL HAPPEN, because they made a commitment.

Questioners initially question all expectations. They need to understand WHY something is being asked, and reject ideas they see as arbitrary or superfluous. Getting questioners to large events like company conventions and leadership events is HUGE for questioners, since they will respect other top-ranking leaders more than you, and will find role models that resonate with them that will make them more likely to follow-through. If you are having difficulty with a questioner, help them see why it makes sense to do what you're asking "the more you engage in the product education page, the more YOUR members will see the posts in their feed, and the more they will see you as a leader!" or "Statistically speaking, over 70% of sales are made after the 4th follow-up attempt."

Rebels can be the most challenging to work with, since they resist both outer and inner expectations. They are also brilliant thinkers and can be good performers if they learn how to work with their tendency. They will blatantly (or at least secretly) refuse to follow through if they feel controlled, even if they know the suggestions are good and sound. Check-in calls and texts can demotivate them, so carefully ask what they have found helped them follow through in the past. Often, rebels (who find their own tendency very difficult to live with sometimes) learn to 'hack' their own resistance impulses and find ways to game-ify or make it more rewarding for themselves. They thrive with flexibility and being trusted to do their work on their own, or even challenged with a difficult task that most people fail to achieve. Often their response: 'watch me!'

Sometimes helping others see the critical importance of accountability requires you to have difficult conversations with them.

Difficult Conversations

Sometimes a leader has to deal directly with accountability issues on a team by having difficult conversations. When members of the team have lost sight of the accountability culture, these conversations are unavoidable. Difficult conversations can be critical to achieving success and therefore can be described as crucial conversations. These can be some of the most challenging conversations we ever have. You may recall from the Communications module what a crucial conversation is.

A crucial conversation is "A discussion between two or more people where (1) stakes are high, (2) opinions vary, and (3) emotions run strong." This definition from the book *Crucial Conversations*[8] certainly describes the kind of conversation needed when a team member is underperforming or struggling. Refer back to the Communication module to review the seven steps to having a difficult discussion.

As the leader, you are responsible for initiating this type of conversation. When something goes wrong, first make it right, then gain understanding as to what happened to prevent it from recurring.

It is during difficult conversations that accountability gets serious. Did they complete their task and achieve their goal? When the answers are no, the conversation needs to be held quickly, with clarity, empathy, and purpose. Done appropriately, these conversations not only lead to corrective actions, they also impart leadership legacy with the other party.

In the best cases, the difficult conversation is with someone with whom there is already a strong relationship and high level of trust. These conversations require the leader to continue to value the individual. Keep in mind these conversations are much easier than they would be if there were no relationship or trust. Those are the most challenging crucial conversations; without a relationship or trust, you have to invest time, focus, and energy to maintain a professional discussion. Remember—there is no room for avoidance here; the conversation must occur.

Even if you don't have a relationship with someone, you can use this approach to have a deep and authentic discussion. You can treat them with respect, encourage them to participate, and listen actively. Having these abilities as a part of your leadership skills means you stand a good chance of influencing them toward success.

Before having a difficult conversation consider the following:

- Plan ahead for the discussion.

- Put the facts together in a reasonable and fair manner.

- Timing is critical to the meeting, don't procrastinate, but don't have it before you're ready.

---

8   *Crucial Conversations* (2002) by Kerry Patterson, Joseph Crenny, Ron McMillan, and Al Switzler *McGraw Hill Books, NY, NY*

- Reflect on the reason for the conversation. Have you explained the impacts of the other person's actions, or lack of actions, to them?

- Did you set the expectation with the other person that they would tell you ahead of time if they were unable to fulfill their commitment?

- Are you maintaining empathy with the other person's position?

- Have you offered to help them solve the problems they are encountering?

Lastly, for those who struggle with conducting these crucial conversations, ask yourself these questions:

- Do I take on too much accountability myself? Be careful of "ownership disease" where you own too many things or own one thing too deeply. Analyze the issue and determine who should be held accountable for the results. If it's you, then stand up and hold yourself accountable; however, if it's another person on the team, sit down with them and discuss their role and the task in question. Show them you can relate, find out why this escaped them, and, together, work on a resolution. Don't take everything on yourself. Have the courage during the crucial conversation to help the other person hold themselves accountable.

- Do you avoid conflict? Some people just plain avoid conflict and, out of fear, can see these difficult conversations as a form of conflict. Instead, see these conversations as a form of mutual respect. Being honest and straightforward with someone shows them that you value them and their input and that you want to partner with them on this process, not dictate to them. Take control of the fear within yourself, and meet with the other person to set the record straight.

Team Accountability

I'm glad the team was accountable to each other...

Kayla was very excited as she hung up the phone! The call with her team had gone great! All of the activities in advance of the event next week at the hotel were really coming together, and everyone was pitching in and taking on new tasks as they arose. She knew the people who had been invited were going to be wowed by the presentation they had planned, and the desserts that would be served afterward sounded out of this world! Just thinking of orange oil on vanilla Creamsicle pie or that peppermint chocolate truffle cupcake made Kayla's mouth water. The dessert idea was so out-of-the-box exciting! Then, it happened...

Kayla – Susan, what do you mean the bakery can't have the desserts ready for our big event? They've had weeks to get ready! The desserts are key to our oil pairing at the end. It's the highlight of the evening!

Susan – Their ovens broke down and won't be fixed in time. It just happened.

Kayla – Can we get another bakery to help us out?

Susan – How can we get them to make the ones we want with such short notice?

Kayla – Can we make them ourselves?

Susan – I'm a pretty good cook, but no way can I make them.

Kayla – I'm getting a sick feeling in my stomach...

Just then the phone rang, and it was Elsa.

Elsa – Hi Kayla! I've been trying to find Susan. Is she with you?

Kayla – She is, but Elsa, have you heard the news about the bakery? I'm so upset!

Elsa – Kayla, could you put me on speaker please? Susan, Janet and I heard about the bakery ovens and we jumped in to help. We knew how important the desserts were, so we had to figure out something. I mean we're all in this together, right?

Susan – We sure are. We're all in big trouble together!

Elsa – That's why I'm calling. I knew Janet's cousin owned a bakery in another town about 2 hours from here. We didn't consider using him at first because of the distance, but with the emergency, we called him right away. And.....he can make ALL of the desserts we had planned! He'll have them to us right on time!

Kayla – Elsa, that's INCREDIBLE NEWS! You and Janet are amazing!

Susan – OMG! I can't believe it! You guys saved us! But, you guys aren't even on the dessert committee, how did you know to help?

Elsa – Well, we're all on the same team, and Janet and I were reviewing the event plan when we heard. We're all responsible to make this the best event ever. We knew other people were counting on us for our tasks, and we had to help Susan out when we heard!

Discussion

A few questions to consider and reflect on:

- What did you think of Kayla's first discussion with Susan?
- Why did Kayla choose to try to solve the problem first?
- What do you think Susan was feeling during their dialogue?
- Why did they not think to bring in the rest of the team?
- How do you think Kayla defined accountability?

- What other questions might you have asked Susan?

- What does accountability mean to you?

- How would you measure the accountability culture within your own team?

Great dive into accountability, but back to Ownership. Fully understanding the nuance of ownership is critical. Now let's look at how you actually create that sense of ownership in yourself and in others.

How Do You Create a Sense of Ownership?

You create a sense of ownership when you apply personal meaning to your work and allow your core values to be engaged and exhibited. There are a lot of sources for personal meaning, and many of them center on pride. In other words, taking pride in your work, your team, your downline, and your business becomes the driver to creating that sense of ownership. It means thinking like a CEO, not an employee. Your fingerprints are all over your work. Taking ownership of the work you do gives you more energy and passion, and enables you to gain more satisfaction from that work. Who doesn't want that?

Another way to create a sense of ownership is to be personally invested and have **"skin in the game."** To do this well, you need to have more than money at risk: you have to have your reputation, your relationships, and sometimes even your future at risk. To sum it up, you are putting your legacy at risk. Your legacy is what people will say about you, your integrity, and your business for years to come. Putting things at risk, like your legacy, generates ownership. When things go badly, it hurts more. When things go well, the feeling is even more triumphant. When you connect ownership to the business, then personal satisfaction rises to new heights. Having skin in the game is where business becomes personal. It's a key component of ownership.

Ownership is not something that someone can confer on you. It's something that you as a leader must choose. You look at an activity or a situation and say, "Okay, this thing is mine, I'm going to make **this** happen!" Taking action and responsibility is a tangible way of creating a sense of ownership.

Owners strive for a goal larger than themselves. They fight every day on behalf of their team and their business. They are the ones who champion, support, and work with the team to motivate them toward their own definition of success.

Ownership of Self

The most fundamental thing that you can own is *yourself*—your internal state as well as your actions. Owning the good and the bad of what you do will inspire others to do the same. People who take ownership admit problems and flaws. They even point them out in themselves because they're not trying to be politically correct—they're trying to make a difference and are playing to win. Each of us makes mistakes, but someone who *owns* their mistakes frees everyone else around them to do the same.

In addition to owning your actions, you must own your decisions. The power you have is tempered by the responsibility for the decisions you make. Take responsibility for your own decisions first.

Now, take this mindset and connect it to your entire business, including your team and downline. While ownership has to start with you, it doesn't gain any impact until you understand what it means to be a part of an effort that is much larger than just you, your actions, and your decisions. Your actions and decisions affect many others, and when others see you acting on behalf of their success, you are seen as an owner!

Ownership of the Enterprise

Another way to think of ownership is to act like you actually own the entire downline. Stay with us here—we know that you don't own all of the businesses in your downline; we're asking you to simply imagine what that might look like. And no, we don't care about whether you recruited someone or someone else did and you are *just* the upline. We're suggesting you try to imagine that the entire downline is your personal business. What would you do and why? Ask yourself, if you owned the entire downline, how happy would you be with the level of service you are providing? Thinking of things in this way is very empowering and, even in difficult situations, can allow you to call upon all of your resources, skills, and abilities.

There is an action that Herb Keller, former CEO of Southwest Airlines, was fond of taking. He made a regular point to show up and work with the crews that cleaned planes, often in the middle of the night. The point was clear. The job of providing a good customer experience trumped everything else at Southwest. Herb owned customer experience.

Making Ownership Happen for YOU

Expand your mindset to see the entire business from the ownership perspective. Seeking areas of ownership avoids a victim mentality. Check out the following list and see how you can take ownership or responsibility for these things/actions, realizing that everyone is different and unique. The *way* you take ownership is likely to be different from the way someone else does.

- Own the definition of success for your business.

- Own each element of what it takes to achieve success.

- Own your influence with the team.

- Own every transaction.

- Be mindful of your attitudes and behaviors.

- Own your customer engagements.

- Own your legacy and the legacy of your business.

What can leaders ask themselves to get the ownership juices flowing? Here are some good questions to get a self-reflective conversation started.

- What areas of my business lack ownership?

- What area does my team and downline think needs to be addressed?

- Why is this business important to each team member on a personal level?

- What would a "total ownership" approach look like to me?

- Why is this business important to me?

- Who owns the success of my business?

- What kinds of changes do I think would make a difference in how others see my business?

- What do I own?

- What am I accountable for?

- What kind of difference in people's lives can I make?

- How can I show my team that I care?
- Is the business better off when I am leading it?

Creating a Sense of Ownership in the Team

As you create a sense of ownership within yourself, it's valuable to create a sense of ownership within your team as well. Others begin to see themselves as "co-owners" with you. How do you do that? First and foremost, it's through the development of solid relationships. As you care about and connect with the team, they will see the ownership within you exhibited frequently. The deeper your relationships go, the more your team will see themselves as partners and co-owners.

Pause and reflect a moment—this co-ownership idea is a BIG deal! When you are able to help your team and downline recognize that we are all owners and partners *together*, everyone's world will be rocked! This is a fundamental component of ownership in our Downline Leadership world: Each of our successes affects the success of someone else. No one is an island, and we rise and fall together. The larger your downline gets, the more you will understand this.

When you see your downline as co-owners, it changes everything. It changes the way you talk to them, the way you engage them, the way you treat them, and the way you collaborate with them—because they are your partners. While we want everyone to really own his or her business, no one does this business on their own, hence co-ownership. When you and your team embrace this concept, everyone's business benefits and there is no limit to what you can accomplish together.

As powerful as relationships are, we also want to connect ownership to the other components of the Leadership Engine. Establishing solid credibility with the team helps the team to see you as the leader, someone worth following, and part of that bigger effort. This begins the cycle of creating a sense of ownership within the team members. As you build deeper and stronger relationships, they see your ownership in action and they begin to trust you more. Earning their trust is a cornerstone to helping the team believe in you. When you have the trust of your team, this empowers them to begin making personal ownership decisions, knowing that you have their backs. Finally, there is influence. Once you have established credibility, developed a relationship, and earned trust, you should be in a position to gain and exert influence. As you model ownership-minded actions, you influence the team to also model personal ownership behavior and you will have successfully created a sense of ownership within them.

Here are some additional tips to help instill ownership in the team:

- Listen to the team and make sure they are heard.
- Help them to see that we are ALL in it together.
- Empower them and give them opportunities to own actions, tasks, events, and other activities.
- Support them and their decisions.
- Recognize them and their work.
- Explain to them the need for skin in the game.
- Include them in planning.
- Help them to set clear expectations and get buy-in.
- Lead by example.
- Have empathy for them.
- Share ownership (don't delegate, it's you and them working together as co-owners).
- Communicate the big picture.
- Trust the team to own their piece of the downline/business.
- Tie everyone's definition of success to their *why* (the real reason they are in this business).
- Model ownership.
- When building the team, help them to become a part of something bigger than themselves.

How do you know when the team has a sense of ownership?

- They're highly responsive.
- They look ahead.
- They have a high level of commitment.
- They ask, "What can we do together to make a difference?" types of questions.

- They are BIG on customer care.

- They think beyond themselves.

- They have a high quality of work.

Let's ask one more question: "Why do you care about being an owner?"

Why Is Having a Sense of Ownership Important?

The choice of owning one's business is one of the most fundamental and important choices you can make because it impacts so many decisions you make later. The effects of ownership can compound and leverage your leadership in many ways. Let's discuss a few of those ways.

Ownership Exhibits Courage

Making the decision to be the owner takes courage. So often, a business is floating along, simply being managed, and is crying out for ownership. It takes courage to step up, take responsibility, and accept total ownership for all of the elements of the business, the team, and the customer. This courage is seen and respected by all.

Ownership Inspires Confidence and Shows Competency

When people see that you have thought things through, gone above and beyond to deliver, you show your competency. What you say and do is generally not questioned—it's trusted.

Competency also inspires confidence. When an owner demonstrates competence in performance for themselves and their team, others are inspired to have confidence in them. Part of showcasing your competency is demonstrating that you know how to deliver on all of your commitments and understand how to achieve true success.

Ownership calls forth the best in others

There is an old piece of advice given to actors: If you don't care, we don't care. Others care when they see you care—they need to see your passion before they will get engaged. Ownership involves passion. Think of the last time you worked all night creating that Facebook event. Others saw your commitment, dedication, passion, and ownership. How about when the team hit a wall and you held a drawing for the newly announced product you purchased to reward a member of the team? These aren't the only ways to exhibit your passion, but they show the team that you care about them all along the way and through to the end.

In whatever form it takes, the pride of ownership shines through, and when it does, it allows you to call upon the best that's within others.

You Are Not the Boss of Me

The most common problem we see with ownership is people not stepping up and owning it. However, there is another problem—letting ownership go to your head. What do I mean?

Some people take *upline* to mean boss. In other words, "I'm your upline, and I will tell you what to do." Why not? This happens all the time anyway when your downline is constantly asking you what to do. Why not just take on the director role and tell them what to do, what to say, how to do it, and when to do it? Because it doesn't work!

This authoritative command-and-control style of leadership will absolutely not work in the long term. It may *seem* to work in the short term as people take your direction and get things done; however, what happens behind the scenes is another matter. When you're not in the role of coach and are no longer asking open-ended questions, you are showing them you no longer care about their ideas and solutions because you have all the ideas necessary. This strategy burns out quickly as people lose respect for you and soon stop asking you to listen to them because they know all they'll receive from you are directions.

Remember that your team doesn't work for you. People in your downline have their own businesses. While everyone's business is intertwined, and your final results are a result of theirs (and so on down the line), this does not mean it's your business. Wait a second—didn't we just tell you to take ownership over everything? No, we said to take on the *attitude* of ownership.

When you become the boss, you either build a culture of mindless followers or of those who rebel. Neither of these is what you want. Your desire is to build your businesses *together*! You want to create a culture where everyone has the attitude of shared ownership. When you share ownership, everyone has skin in the game and is committed to each other's success. When someone has a tough month, we all have a tough month.

Once ownership is shared, it begins to cascade to everyone's downline. Imagine if we were all owners! In this scenario, no one is the boss of anyone, as we are all co-owners and the team works together to achieve success for all.

You Owned It!

Maya heard the phone ring. She saw it was Laura calling. She let out a big sigh and, against her better judgment, decided to answer the call. She was talking to herself before she answered,

"I really hope that this is not another two-hour call with some problem Laura doesn't know how to solve. I just can't do that today."

Laura: Hi, Maya. Well, corporate messed up on another shipment today!

Maya: I'm sorry to hear that. (Maya thinks of hanging up as Laura whines, but instead, pauses for a moment and reflects on who owns this problem—her, Laura, or corporate?)

Laura: Maya, are you still there?

Maya: Sorry Laura, I was just thinking. (Pause) Laura, let's look at this from an ownership perspective.

Laura: What do you mean? It's corporate's fault. They should fix it.

Maya: I know corporate made a mistake, but whose customer is it?

Laura: Mine, but how can I be responsible for all of corporate's mistakes?

Maya: Whom do you think the customer holds responsible?

Laura: Well me, I guess. But I can't go down to the warehouse and show them how to handle shipping, can I?

Maya: No, it's just a different way to look at things. If you were the customer, wouldn't you want to be totally taken care of and only need one person to talk to? Well, that one person is you. You own the customer relationship and experience. You don't own the delivery process or the warehouse, but you are responsible for finding out what it will take to correct the situation and make the customer happy. You. Laura, I'm talking about being an owner. This is your business. Find out what corporate can do to fix this and get it done. You don't need me to make your calls for you, you can do that. I'm an owner just like you, and when I don't know something, I go get the answers. It's time for you to do the same thing.

Laura: But, but, but, I don't think I can do it! I mean, whom should I call? Where do I start? You've always done this for me.

Maya: I know you can do this, and I've got your back. First, start by calling this number for support and then go from there. If you have any challenges, get back to me.

Laura: I guess I can do this...

(Two weeks later... Laura calls Maya.)

Laura: Hey there! I wanted to let you know that I got that whole shipping problem solved!

Maya: That's great news! How did you do that?

Laura: It turns out that corporate had two different addresses for my client and kept shipping to the wrong one. It took several calls to find the mistake, but corporate was apologetic, sent the client an extra oil for their trouble, and thanked me for finding a glitch in their system. The client was very appreciative of my extra effort and has referred me to a friend of theirs who's interested in buying a kit. That's a pretty solid result for making a few extra calls!

Maya: Sounds like you did the work and got it to happen. I'd say you owned it!

Discussion

What do you think of Laura's exhibition of ownership? Seems easy enough to do, but how many of us have folks who will not make that one additional call? What do you think of Maya's use of coaching and mentoring? What might you have done differently if you had been Maya?

The Path Forward

In this module, we explored ownership and what it means for a leader to lay claim to a business as being completely theirs.

We examined the difference between accountability and ownership, and how ownership is an internal and intangible act of choice. Owners will hold themselves accountable for everything, not just for those things that can be measured.

It's the leader's privilege and opportunity to take ownership of a business and to make ownership happen not only for themselves, but also for those on their team. It's all about creating that sense of ownership.

We discussed how to go about creating an Accountability Culture and the nuances associated with that task. As the owner of your business, the leader embraces the responsibility of creating this culture within his or her team.

We looked at how ongoing dialogue regarding accountability helps drive effective execution.

We touched on conducting the difficult conversations for which the leader is responsible.

In the end, having ownership of a business will pull the best from you and from others. It significantly increases the chances for higher levels of success. There aren't many things more important than ownership, and that's why we say...

Just OWN it!

Action Required

In preparation for our next group meeting, please complete the exercise on the next page.

Discussion Framework

Use this page to capture your preliminary thoughts about this module's content. Each quadrant has questions that are provided to help stimulate your thoughts and reflections. This is not a quiz and there are no wrong answers. It is an opportunity to deepen self-awareness, so capture whatever seems appropriate to you.

	INTERNAL	EXTERNAL
INDIVIDUAL	**Reflect** What did you read about this week that caught your eye and caused you to reflect? Where have I enabled my team Instead of empowering them?	**Adopt** What would you like to adopt as a going-forward behavior or process that you picked up from this week's module? Ownership is Making Sure everything gets done pg 87 & 88 Questions
GROUP	**Inquire** What question would you like to ask the group concerning the topic(s) in the module?	**Share** What insight, principle, or leadership precept did you want to share with the group?

INTUITION

Some call it a hunch. Others call it a gut feeling, or discernment, or even an instinct or inkling. We call it *intuition*, and we believe this leadership competency to be one of the most important skills in your arsenal. Intuition can accelerate your leadership effectiveness like no other skill. Intuition enables you to jump ahead in your decision-making. It's the ability to take limited hard data and develop a strategy to move forward—while others are still looking for more information. It's the skill of knowing whom to recruit, who will do the business, who should be placed in which leg, and into whom you should invest. It's hearing what's *not* being said. It's that feeling in your stomach that you need to turn right even when that road looks less (okay, a lot less) traveled. It's *knowing*.

In this module, we'll explore why Intuition is important for a Downline Leader and introduce some tools to develop yours.

Module Overview

In completing this module, you will

- Understand the nature of intuition—what it is, what it's not, and its direct connection to leadership and decision-making.

- Learn how to build and grow your intuition skills.

- Review the relationship between intuition and influence.

- Discover ways to recover when your intuition fails you.

What Is Intuition?

Intuition is the ability to combine the hard data of the physical world with the soft data of the emotional world and make a decision to move forward. Intuition connects the reasoning (left) side of your brain to the emotional (right) side. Intuition bridges the gap between instinct and rational thought. Unfortunately, it's frequently misunderstood, and many people think that using your intuition is just *guessing*. However, we contend that you are in fact making data-driven decisions; it's simply that the data comes from a different place (your emotional side) than you're accustomed to gathering it from. Intuition can help you produce exceptional results in a shorter time and with less information!

People who are proficient in using their intuition process information in a parallel manner rather than processing it sequentially. These individuals see patterns where others don't. They combine their insight into these patterns with their experience and collected emotional data to come up with a decision or a direction. Intuition tends to be informal, subjective, qualitative, dynamic, and flexible.

How can this translate to the real world? Let's say you're talking to someone about a possible change of direction during a team meeting. You sense that they're concerned about the new strategy and you ask them solid coaching questions. With each answer, you gain both tangible information (their answers) as well as intangible signals (their body language, speech nuance and tone, and reactions from others in the meeting). It's your intuition that combines these two data types to create a decision for action.

When do you need intuition?

There are many situations where your intuition can help you as a leader. Here are a few examples:

- You need a quick decision! When fully engaged with your intuition skills, you're able to make decisions faster and with less information. Put another way, if you wait until you have enough data to make a decision, there is a very good chance that the decision will be obsolete because things will have changed while you were gathering the data. For example, you're using your intuition when you are able to assess a situation instantly and come up with a Facebook post that addresses the current market opportunity before anyone else—and even more importantly, before the market shifts to something different.

- The problem you're facing is very complex, ambiguous, or not easily understood. Regular information is not nearly enough to help you with this situation. You need your intuition to piece together some really difficult-to-comprehend principles and data.

- You're in new territory. You have no experience, nor do you have any counsel or advice. You have to go with your gut.

Attributes of Intuition

Intuition comes with many strengths and benefits, including the following:

Intuition as Empowerment

Intuition frequently empowers you when you're reflecting on who you are and what your values are. It's your intuition that brings your self-awareness to your thought process, empowering you to say, "I know who I am and I will go this way!" Your intuition can be of immeasurable value during this personal reflection exercise. No one knows you better than yourself. You can take personality tests and skill assessments to help collect data about yourself; however, it's your intuition that interprets this data and combines it with your own reflection to craft a balanced reflection of who you are and what you're great at doing. Armed with this insight, you're empowered to push ahead to make significant strides in achieving success.

Intuition as Strength Finder

Intuition can also help identify your strengths. Using your intuition to hone in on your true strengths empowers you to be more than good at something—it enables you to be *great* at it. There's no more wasted energy trying things that are likely to fail. Instead, your intuition tells you to invest time into your strengths, and, in fact, your intuition tends to be the clearest in the areas of your strengths. The confidence that comes from knowing those strengths helps you achieve your goals.

Intuition as Charter of New Directions

Intuition helps you to blaze new opportunities, go beyond where you've gone before, jump out of that box, and produce amazing results. If the circumstance or situation is new to you, your intuition will help. In new situations, you have little experience or data from which to pull. Time to use your intuition! "Which path do I take—the right one or the left one?" Your intuition says, "Go left." Check yourself—does that feel right? If so, then go for it! Later in this module, we'll talk about what to do when your intuition fails you (no one, and we mean no one, is perfect). In the meantime, invest in taking intuitive risks, and keep moving forward. It's the only way to achieve exceptional results. And what better example can we use than ranking up! Intuition helps you jump ahead, and isn't that what ranking up is? You will have to do something new and different to rank up. Your best tool to rank up is obvious... intuition.

Intuition as a Spark of Creativity

Many people claim they are not creative. This is simply not true. We all have pieces of creativity inside of us; we just don't let them out. Your intuition can help in this area as well. For example, let's say you're fearful of giving presentations. Go ahead—try to imagine doing a 101 class to a group of people. If you let your fears, self-doubt, and inhibitions take over, it's highly likely the presentation will go poorly. Now, close your eyes and imagine that same presentation coming across in an incredibly powerful way. Let your intuition fuel your creativity in what to say and how to say it. Now, take that inner picture and schedule a class. Prepare for it, do the work, and take the risk of putting your intuition on the line. As you're presenting, get your internal radar out and look at the crowd. Are they responding to you or not listening? If they're losing focus, change it up. Go in another direction. Interrupt yourself and ask a question to gauge where they are. Listen to the answer and any hidden messages, and self-correct to a new line of discussion. It's not easy being this self-aware and in tune with our intuition, but with practice it gets easier and easier.

Intuition—Innate or Learned?

As with most skills, intuition has both an innate and a learned element to it. We've all met people who seem more intuitive, blessed with a natural gift, and there is some truth to that. However, the majority of the time, the intuition you see in action is a result of growing, fostering, failing, reflecting, and learning how to read your intuition and take action based on your gut. We ALL have intuition, it's up to us as leaders to recognize our intuition and to grow it.

Quick and Slow Intuition

People tend to be either quick intuitive or slow intuitive. Neither is right or wrong, and both have their pros and cons, which leaders have to manage. When you are quick intuitive, you tend to make decisions very fast without a lot of data. This can leapfrog you ahead of everyone else. Unfortunately, most quick intuitive people don't spend any time evaluating their few failures. If they were to have just asked one more open-ended question, they might have gotten the data they needed.

Slow intuitive people tend to take longer to make decisions as they gather more emotional data, but when they do make a decision, it is almost always right on. Unfortunately for slow intuitive people, their challenge is to know when to gather more data or when to make the call with the data they have.

Let's discuss how you enhance your intuition skills.

How Do You Grow and Use Your Intuition?

It's time to engage those intuition muscles! Don't let fear hold you back from taking the necessary risks to free your intuitive skills. As with coaching, you can grow and cultivate your intuition skills. Here are some ideas and tips on how to learn to recognize and believe in your inner voice.

Trust Yourself

Intuition can only be used when you trust yourself. To trust yourself, you have to know who you are. This comes from a continuous investment into your self-awareness. Ask yourself—*What are my values? What is my why (your purpose for doing your business)? Why do I care about others?* When you have a good grasp on who you are, as well as on these other questions, it's time to trust yourself. Trust that your judgments, opinions, and decisions will generally be in the interest of you, your family, your team, and your business. Trust your feelings and intuition. If you don't trust yourself, it becomes hard to contextualize the emotional data your intuition is collecting. It becomes nearly impossible to balance the hard and soft data to make solid decisions— and you simply won't *know* which direction to go.

The largest obstacle to having effective intuition is self-doubt. The greatest weapon against self-doubt is trust in yourself. Believe in yourself! Look in the mirror and smile, because that person you're looking at is talented, smart, and trustworthy! Now, let that self-doubt just fade away.

Use All of Your Senses

When trying to use your intuition, you need to put all of your senses into play. Did you hear that small gasp at the end of the table when something controversial was said? Did you see Mary shrug her shoulders ever so slightly when a new topic was brought up? Did you sense how nervous Jane was when you shook her hand? Did you smell which oil was diffusing in the corner? What does that tell you about the mood of the room? Your intuition uses all of these data points and others as you go through the discussion. While intuition is sometimes referred to as the sixth sense, it helps if you use the first five.

Observe EVERYTHING

You need to take in everything around you to provide your intuition with data. However, before you go into data overload, figure out a way to capture what you're going through. Keep a journal of your intuitive moments. Record your emotional insights; track all of those times when your intuition was right on, as well as those times when it wasn't. What were the circumstances surrounding your insight? How did you get there? Ask yourself these questions and write your answers in your *Intuition Journal* (a tool many leaders use to record their intuitive moments). This single action will propel your intuition forward. Observe it all.

Recognize and Embrace Your Emotions

Earlier we said that intuition connects your reasoning to your emotions. However, that connection can't happen if you don't acknowledge, recognize, search inside of, and embrace your emotions. Your job is to stay grounded, be present, and experience the emotion you're going through. Bring that awareness to the situation, and let that emotion be a balanced part of the intuitive process. Your emotions will always be a filter for your intuition, but don't let them overtake the intuition process.

Because emotions frequently filter and inhibit your intuition, you must be on the lookout for when emotions are in play. Emotions are indicators, not dictators, of your actions. Also be careful when the relationships are deep and long (like with family members), where emotions will most definitely have an impact on your intuition's effectiveness.

For example, let's say you've just recruited someone to the business and you're very confident they're going to succeed. If you let this confidence overwhelm you, you'll miss some of the signals when they begin to struggle, and you won't be as responsive to their needs as you should be. Your intuition is saying, "They've got this," because you recruited them and predicted success. It doesn't mean that your intuition was wrong in recruiting them; it simply means you've let this emotion color your present intuition too much. Be balanced.

Always Stay True to Your Values

This one is related to the aspect of "*Trust yourself*" that was mentioned earlier. The values you hold dear are part of who you are. Your intuition is an extension of those same values. Growing your intuition takes courage as you take more risks. One of the things that enables you to have courage is knowing that when you're taking a risk by trusting your intuition, your intuitive feeling will be coming from your value system. In fact, if your intuition indicates an action that's not based on your values, then it's likely you're getting a false signal. Let that one go and refocus on your values. They won't let you down when you're basing a decision on your intuition.

Listen to Your Heart

When you're really focused on growing and using your intuition, listen not only to your gut (your inner voice), but also listen to your heart. What's your heart saying? Have you actually asked yourself what you should do? Or are you simply going along, collecting the hard data, waiting for all the planets to align, and running the next play out of the playbook? Still yourself, get quiet, and ask yourself what you should do. This takes some effort. Turn off all the distractions, inputs, and noise. Stop asking the counsel of everyone, including the cab driver. Look inward. Who better to ask than yourself? Who knows what's more important to you than YOU? Listen to your heart.

Reflection and Self-Awareness

When you get quiet, practice reflection. You've got all of this emotional data and your intuition is sorting through it. However, if you don't reflect on what you've learned along the way, there will be no context for your intuition to act upon. Look backward to past events and take an emotional read of your experience. Apply that insight to your current situation. Bring your self-awareness up a notch and get ready to ride your intuition to the next level.

Connect with Others

In the Leadership Engine, we emphasized how important it is to connect with others to establish your credibility, develop relationships, earn trust, and gain influence. Now, you get another benefit from that connection—higher levels of intuition. When you're gathering all of the emotional data, another critical filter is the level of connection you have with others. The deeper the connection, the more accurate the data will be for your intuition to act upon. For instance, you'll know that the shrug from Mary means a different thing than the shrug from Susan. Let's not forget that the reason we're using our intuition is to make decisions that help the team. Those decisions only become more effective and powerful as your connection with the team becomes more important and meaningful to you and others.

Review Your Results

Let's say you have had an intuitive moment and you've documented it in your Intuition Journal. Now, it's time to read that journal, evaluate your successes and failures, and learn from them. Test your hunches against what happened. Did you read the team right? Did they receive your message in the way you intended? Did you achieve your goal? We've discussed Feedback Loops and their value several times already. This would be an outstanding time to use them as you evaluate your intuitive skills and where to grow them.

Ask yourself—did you move too fast or too slow? Did you have the right intuitive insight, but were late in using it and lost the moment? Did you let your emotions mask the intuition data coming in? Reflect, reflect, and reflect. When you think you have a handle on what went wrong, reflect one more time to confirm.

We touched on influence above, now let's go a little deeper to understand how intuition and influence work together.

How Intuition and Influence Work Together

Using your intuition to read the room—to assess the interests and concerns of everyone in it—is a tremendous source of influence. Knowing the room is more than not being caught flat-footed by a question—it's being ahead of the question. By intuitively anticipating what comes next, you demonstrate that you understand not just the demands and details of the topic, but also the needs of everyone in the room, and you are working to meet them. Your intuition is guiding your emotional read of the room and its participants. You know where it *could* go, and it's time to influence the room to go there. Intuition and influence work together to help you lead stronger and faster.

Here are some questions to consider as you use your intuition in concert with your influence.

- What's the emotional level of the participants in the room?

- What are the unspoken agendas of the participants?

- Who is your ally and who needs more information?

- What's the flow of the conversation? What undercurrents are at play?

- Which person is distracting you?

- How are you connecting with each person and addressing his or her concerns?

- Who needs to feel heard and understood?

In the Leadership Engine module, we said that leadership is influence. It seems to reason that when we use our intuition effectively to increase our influence, then our leadership increases. When guiding your team, your intuition is helping you to know the best course of action to take, while the influence you've gained makes you *that* leader who will be able to take the team there!

Let's look further into those times your intuition failed you and what you can do about it.

What To Do When Your Intuition Fails You

It happens—your intuition wasn't right. You misread a situation or a person. You made a decision that didn't pan out. How could this happen?

- Your emotions got out of hand. We talked earlier about how easy it is for your emotions to cloud your intuition. Sometimes it's because you're suppressing an emotion that you need to have at your disposal to better interpret the moment. At other times, you're so overwhelmed by an emotion, like being mad, that no matter what's said you read everything through the filter of your anger.

- You had preconceived opinions. You went into the situation already believing you knew what was going to happen. You didn't listen to new input or new emotional data. You based your actions solely on past performance or past intuitions instead of being in the present and reading today's inputs.

- You refused to believe your intuition. You thought it was a crazy idea, even though it lined up with your values. You simply didn't see yourself taking this action when your intuition was trying to tell you to act.

- You won't forgive yourself for the last error. Now you're gun shy. You had an embarrassing experience when you misread a situation and it was painful. You don't care what your intuition is telling you now—you're not going to listen to it! This is your self-doubt creeping back.

- You acted too quickly and the emotional data were insufficient or inaccurate. Because you acted too quickly, you neglected to be open to alternative decisions.

- You have good intuition in one area, but that led you to become overconfident and to use your intuition in an area in which you weren't familiar.

What do you do? Stop, reflect, and take a breath. Then, try one or more of these actions.

- First, apologize to anyone you may have hurt with your intuitive decision.

- Get your journal out. Look at all the times your intuition led to a better decision that benefitted you and/or the team. Build your confidence back up. Like any soft skill, you can have failure. That doesn't mean you give up on intuition!

- Turn your emotions around and get positive. While many of your emotions are filters that inhibit your intuition, there are times that your emotions can also channel your intuition. Find your balance. You can do this!

- Open your senses back up and begin collecting new emotional data. What does it tell you? Reflect, evaluate, feel, and pull the trigger again. There's no mystery here. You simply have to trust yourself, get over the mistakes, and accept that they will happen again. Everything is fluid, and things change all the time. Adjust, change, grow, make decisions, and learn from your mistakes.

- Take ownership of your intuition. Once you've taken ownership, you give your intuition permission to work.

Here's an approach that author Gary Klein (*Power of Intuition*, New York: Currency/Doubleday [2004], by way of a *Forbes* article on Aug 5, 2013 by Cheryl Conner) describes as a decision model that uses intuition at the core. It's a good resource to use after a failure.

- **Listen better**—Improved listening will ensure getting more of the situational information you need. The stronger the pattern, the more likely your intuition can provide a solution that meshes well with the problem at hand.

- **Reflect on a decision before implementing it**—Look for areas where emotions might be distorting your perception of the current situation. Get trusted advisors to help identify whether your perception may be clouded by the desires and emotions you feel.

- **Examine your beliefs**—Are they based on reliable facts and evidence?

- **Communicate**—You should do your best to explain the reasoning behind your intuition to the others with whom you work. If you don't, they will likely work to undermine its implementation.

- **Learn to recognize and interpret your emotions**—Your emotions are valuable signals of previous patterns and experiences. If you can learn what they're pointing you to, you'll be better prepared to know when you can count on your intuition to appropriately lead the way.

- **Create the right learning environment**—Intuitive decision-making gets better with practice. If you can work in (and create) an environment that provides tolerance for you and your team, you will progressively make better intuitive choices.

- **Use situational assessments and case studies**—Just as is done in universities and military settings, studying the previous outcomes of other similar situations can improve the decision-making process for you and can help to build patterns for your intuition to follow.

Don't forget that the number one reason our intuition fails us is self-doubt. For example, you've lost your favorite pen. It can be in one of three places. Your intuition tells you it's in location one, but you figure you'll check locations two and three to be sure. This is self-doubt! Instead, go to location one first! Be confident, believe in yourself and your intuition, and be the leader you were meant to be!

Let's explore why intuition is helpful in situational leadership.

Role Agility: The BIG Reason to Use Intuition

Okay, we saved the best for last. **The biggest reason to develop your intuition is to help you know which leadership role you should be using, and when to shift roles.** This concept of situational leadership is one of the foundations of the Downline Leadership program. To be an effective leader, you have to know when to direct, teach, mentor, or coach. We can't think of a better way to *know* this than through your intuition.

You are speaking with someone on your team and you sense that the tone of the discussion has shifted. You had been in coach mode, asking some great open-ended questions when the other person started to get frustrated. It's intuition time! Does your intuition tell you that you need to stay in the coaching role and ask, "Why are you getting frustrated?" or do you need to shift to the teacher role and say something like, "Let me show you what I was asking you about." Choosing the wrong role in this moment can impact the relationship. What to do? Follow your intuition!

A moment earlier, your intuition had already told you that the conversation needed a change. What is your intuition telling you now? Which role feels right for the moment? Use empathy. If you were the other person, which role would you prefer to hear right now?

Each of the leadership roles (director, teacher, mentor, coach) has its place. You may recall we espouse the practice of "*coach first*" so you can gather data for your intuition to act on. Once you've gotten those data, then choose the role and take action! The more your intuition grows, the faster you will be able to choose which role to be in. You'll find yourself saying the right thing at the exact right time to help the other person through their challenges and to continually improve your relationships with them.

What if I choose the wrong role? Think back to the section where you learned what to do when your intuition fails you. Change roles quickly, since you're in a live conversation and you don't want to hurt or offend the other person. Get back in their trust fast!

Use your intuition with role agility effectively and you will be *that* leader whom everyone will want to follow. Here's a story where intuition is on center stage.

Intuition Isn't Always Easy

Beth was really excited after having recruited three people to buy kits these past two weeks. It was time to place them in the best leg she could, strategically structuring her downline. But, how could she know which leg to put them in? How could she be certain which one might become another business person? Time for intuition!

The first person Beth had recruited was Janet, and this one was a no-brainer. Janet had actually chased Beth down to be in the business and already had several leads on kits. Beth knew exactly which leg to put her in (Shauna's leg) where she would fit in well with that team. Beth's intuition seemed very sure on this one. Flash forward six months and Beth had been right on. Janet was already an Executive and well on her way to hitting Silver. She had merged well with Shauna's team, and had been a self-starter and passionate businessperson from the start. All the signals that Beth's intuition had picked up on had rung true.

The second person Beth had recruited was June, and again, Beth knew right away where to place her. June wasn't very interested in the business and showed that from the beginning. She simply loved her oils and wanted them for her family. Beth placed her in a leg that needed some product sales and was never disappointed. Looking ahead six months, June was still a wonderful, paying customer and had recently given some hints that she was thinking about starting the business. Wouldn't that be the icing on the cake?

The third person Beth had recruited was Jody, and Beth felt very strongly that Jody was going to be a superstar just like Janet was. Many of the signals were the same between the two, with one exception. Jody was engaged to get married, and became pregnant soon after the wedding. This changed Jody's short-term priorities, and Beth's intuition hadn't seen that coming at all. Flash forward twelve months, and Jody never came back to the business, as she spent all of her time with her new daughter.

Beth reflected on all three of the placements and saw how her intuition had almost been right on. She had seen patterns that were familiar to her, and she'd had the strong sense from talking to all three that she understood their whys and where they wanted to go. The only one she missed on was Jody, and it wasn't that her intuition was wrong; other events changed Jody's why. By reflecting on each of these, Beth was able to grow her intuition and place her experiences in context for the next recruit she was getting ready to place.

Discussion

Notice how Beth used her intuition to handle a very difficult decision, placing a new member in the right leg with the right level of support for that person to be successful. Her intuitive decisions had come from many other experiences and more than a few failures in placement. What kinds of questions and signals would you look for from a new potential business person? How would you recover from someone who you thought was going to rock the business, but then walked away?

The Path Forward

In this module, we covered how intuition is the key to taking your leadership to the next level. By bridging the gap between your rational mind and your emotional mind, you're able to use your intuition to make better decisions, faster.

We demystified what intuition is and how you can grow and use it. By listening to your heart, connecting to others, and trusting your values as well as yourself, your intuition will become more refined and valuable to you as a leader.

The module reviewed ways that your intuition can fail you and what you can do to recover and begin using your intuition again.

Lastly, we tied intuition to role agility and how you can take advantage of your unique intuitive insights to take the role that your team and business needs.

Action Required

In preparation for our next group meeting, please complete the exercise on the last page.

Discussion Framework

Evaluated experience is the best teacher

Use this page to capture your preliminary thoughts about this module's content. Each quadrant has questions that are provided to help stimulate your thoughts and reflections. This is not a quiz and there are no wrong answers. It is an opportunity for deep self-awareness, so capture whatever seems appropriate to you.

Yellow is question

	INTERNAL	EXTERNAL
INDIVIDUAL	**Reflect** What did you read about this week that caught your eye and caused you to reflect? Self Doubt is #1 Reason Intuition fails	**Adopt** What would you like to adopt as a going-forward behavior or process that you picked up from this week's module? Learn to Rec & Interp emotions Study previous outcomes to help w/ decision Making
GROUP	**Inquire** What question would you like to ask the group regarding the topic(s) in the module? Read a Room but Know how to shift gears Roles	**Share** What insight, principle, or leadership precept would you like to share with the group?

Watch people & observe a check in recent visual before (class) on how I want it to go

OVERCOMING CHALLENGES

Challenges are an unavoidable part of any business and determining how to deal with them successfully is a hallmark of a leader. We define overcoming challenges as *removing the obstacles, ambiguity, and issues that hinder progress.*

We are talking about challenges that defy easy solutions and crisp answers—challenges that might involve conflict between team members and challenges for which there may be no right answers. These are *not* the basic, everyday items, such as solving problems or fixing simple issues. You already do this on a daily basis. The challenges we're referring to are big and thorny. It takes a true leader with significant skill and insight to overcome these challenges.

This module will provide the foundation for a deep and rich dialogue on the topic of overcoming challenges.

Module Overview

As a result of experiencing this module you will:

- Consider different types of challenges from the perspective of a leader.

- Examine your choices when deciding how to handle a challenge.

- Contemplate which techniques to add to your leadership skillset to deal with challenges.

What are Challenges?

Challenges are items that hinder your team's progress toward success. We want to reinforce this because of how easy it is to lose sight of your goals, especially in the day-to-day, head-down attention to your business. As we'll discuss later, keeping your focus on each of your team member's definition of success is a terrific way to overcome challenges and become that "go to" leader.

In this section, we will identify five major types of challenges and illustrate how they relate to leadership. Later, in the "What is Overcoming?" section, we'll present some thoughts on how to approach these challenges. The major challenge types are:

- The Success Challenge
- The Unknown Challenge
- The Phantom Challenge
- The People Challenge
- The Ambiguity Challenge

The Success Challenge

Not having a clear definition of success is perhaps the #1 challenge you will face as a leader. Remember, the definition of success is attaining the target or goal that the person is shooting for. It could be hitting the next rank/level or hosting a successful event. Without a clear target, you'll struggle to engage and help your teammates. You'll find it difficult to help people hold themselves accountable without a clear goal, and you won't have much of an impact.

Note—we're reinforcing the importance of the definition of success because not having a clear definition will present a significant challenge for you and your team; you will need to have your definition in the forefront of your mind as you examine the other challenges that come your way. As we'll soon discuss, evaluating the meaning and significance of a challenge *as it relates to the definition of success* is an important step for a leader to take.

The Unknown Challenge

It's difficult to overcome a challenge that you don't know you have! High on the list of frustrating things for any leader is discovering a problem when it's too late to do anything about it. Not only is the original problem an issue, but so is learning that people didn't raise it sooner. Whether it's an issue of trust, communications, or another reason for less than total disclosure, leaders that are kept in the dark have their work cut out for them.

The unknown challenge is potentially the most common problem you will encounter due to the nature of your downline. As your business grows, so does your downline and the number of people with whom you may not have a relationship. This environment breeds unknown challenges as people may not communicate quickly, effectively, or consistently about the challenges they are facing. It all comes back to relationships. When you or your leaders do not have relationships with members of their downline, unknown challenges are sure to arise involving any number of issues.

The Phantom Challenge

In some ways, this is the opposite of The Unknown Challenge. The Phantom Challenge is the one that presents itself as a real, solid, and significant problem, yet it's not real. For example, let's say you posted something you considered really important, and no one responded to the post in the first 24 hours. Your immediate thought was that the post was poorly written. However, on the second day, the replies went crazy. It turns out that the post had affected many people, but they were thinking of how to respond. It wasn't a real challenge. Another indication that you might have a phantom challenge is in how it shows up. Instead of discovering it on your own, it's usually brought to your attention by someone on the team or even your customer. Think of the cry of "wolf" from the fable "The Boy Who Cried Wolf" as a Phantom Challenge—at least, until the wolf finally does show up!

Phantom Challenges are difficult to address because of their nature. This is especially true if another team member brought one to you and it seems real; you have to spend energy and attention dealing with it until you know it's a Phantom. After all, one of these times it may be the wolf.

One other reason to look into Phantom Challenges is that sometimes the phantom is masking another challenge that is very real. Later, we'll look at how holding a challenge up to the definition of success can help us determine if it is a Phantom.

The People Challenge

When people don't get along with each other they frequently prevent you and your team from getting work done. They include things that prevent people from communicating clearly, connecting genuinely, or executing effectively. Conventional obstacles, such as tactical issues and risks, are a big part of management, and you deal with them all the time. The people challenges we are talking about here are leadership issues that deal with the way people relate and interact with each other.

As the leader, part of your role is creating an environment where others can work together so that they can be productive, effective, and deliver success. It's not your role to do all the work, but it is your responsibility to remove obstacles so others can continue to make progress.

The Ambiguity Challenge

Ambiguity is an ongoing challenge that can plague teams. Ambiguity is uncertainty or lack of clarity, and it usually means the path forward is unclear. For example, imagine one of your teammates calls with a problem. The first time you listen to them, you just don't understand the problem. You ask clarifying questions, but it gets even fuzzier. You go through another round of questions, and, just when you think you've finally got it, the other person says that's not it. You've now spent 30 minutes and haven't a clue what the problem is.

Ambiguity causes tension and conflict on teams and in your business because of the time element. Your business requires decisions to be made and outcomes to be achieved at a certain pace, but when ambiguity rears its head, it slows everything down while you try to figure it out.

Now that we've explored the major types of leadership challenges you may face, let's examine what it means to overcome them.

What is Overcoming?

In this section, we propose an approach for overcoming challenges that uses the lens of leadership. You may decide this approach works for you, or you may find pieces of it that can be incorporated into your own personal approach. One point to keep in mind when looking at this approach is that it takes a measure of courage and confidence from the leader in order to be used.

An Approach to Overcoming Challenges

When dealing with a challenge and determining the nature of the challenge, we like to use open-ended coaching questions to help frame the discussion. Here's a series of questions you can use to stimulate your thinking around the challenge:

- What is my reaction to it?

- How well defined is it?

- Why do I believe this is a challenge?

- How do I plan on overcoming the challenge?

- How would a leader overcome it?

- Who else could or should overcome it?

- If it's someone else's, how can I help *him or her* overcome it?

- What do your values tell you?

- What is my level of sensitivity and empathy to those involved?

What is my reaction toward it?

What happens when a challenge surfaces? How do you react? Are you ecstatic, showing a big smile and your appreciation to the person who brings a challenge to your attention? Not exactly, right?

Think about how you feel when others **don't** share issues, obstacles, and challenges with you. If it's because they're proactively solving them on their own, that's phenomenal. If it's because they didn't think it important to bring you into the loop, that's a credibility problem. If they don't bring challenges to you because they're afraid of how you might react, you may have trust issues or perhaps self-confidence issues.

Notice we're talking about how you *first* react to hearing about a challenge. That's because a big part of overcoming challenges is not about the challenge itself—**it's about how you respond to it**. What makes for an effective leader is the attitude they have toward challenges.

Leaders don't see themselves as victims of circumstance, but instead **choose a positive attitude** as they face adversity. They understand that part of being a leader is to "see around the corner" and be prepared for unexpected challenges. They find that place of being grounded and centered before responding.

Leaders recognize that the facts of the challenge are not going to change, and neither will the external factors. Truly, the only thing that the leader is able to control is their personal attitude about the challenge.

Equally important is this fact: how you internalize the challenge dictates not only how you will respond but also what others will see. Do you generally see challenges as disruptions, or do you see them as opportunities for learning and growth? The confidence (depth, strength) of your leadership is seen through your response to challenges.

If you see the challenge as an opportunity to add value where others could not, then your team may also see it as an opportunity. If you approach a challenge with a "woe is me" attitude, then your team will be downcast every time something doesn't go according to plan. All of this rides on *your* attitude.

In choosing their attitude, leaders understand a core principle: A bad reaction can potentially multiply the challenge; therefore, it's important to model the right behaviors.

How well defined is it

This is where ambiguity decides to crash the party. Sometimes the challenge itself is ambiguous or sometimes an otherwise straightforward challenge becomes exceptionally difficult because of the ambiguity surrounding it.

Remember that the opposite of ambiguity is clarity. Therefore, when others are struggling with ambiguity, your role may be to help them reach a level of clarity that allows them to function effectively. Clarity is accomplished through mining the facts and removing assumptions as much as possible. Keep on asking questions, and be patient. Perhaps the other person is not good at communicating, or perhaps the issue is complex and difficult to describe. Either way, stick with it, and don't get frustrated. Find your balance between overreacting, inaction, and patience.

Your role as the leader requires the highest levels of ambiguity tolerance. After all, if you're uneasy about an ambiguous situation, your team will pick up on it and will begin to emulate your anxiousness.

Ambiguity tolerance is like a muscle; you can exercise it in one setting, and it will be there for you when you need it later in another setting. One way you can work your ambiguity muscle is to deliberately put yourself in situations where you don't know the answer to something. Perhaps you can drive somewhere and get purposefully lost. See what happens. How does it feel? What awareness do you have about your own level of ambiguity tolerance?

Why do I believe this is a challenge?

As previously mentioned, sometimes you're presented with "phantoms" that turn out to not be challenges at all. As a leader, your role may be to identify whether or not a challenge truly merits your full-blown attention. Remember to dig deep enough to find any challenges that may be hidden under the surface. Use open-ended questions to uncover the real issue. Phantom challenges are not the same as ambiguous challenges, although both require you to dig into them to figure out what is wrong.

How do I plan on overcoming the challenge?

Once you have enough clarity on the challenge, it's important to evaluate whether or not the challenge matters for success. Some challenges are indeed full-blown challenges, but they may not be directly relevant to success.

This is where having clarity around the definition of success is key; with a well-defined challenge, you can hold it up to the definition of success and determine if they're related. Most of us are problem solvers, and we have a tendency to solve the problem without carefully evaluating it against the current definition of success. That's where the leader steps in, asking open-ended questions that get at the root of the process. Here's a short list of tips for dealing with challenges:

- Pause and assess the challenge before taking any action.
- Break it apart and determine which pieces need to be addressed.
- Determine what is fact and what is assumption.
- Deal with the challenge as quickly as possible.
- Take it offline if necessary.

Don't let challenges become a distraction to your delivery of success. Remember that we are striving for personal and team success (the reaching of their goals), and these challenges can be in our way. It's your job as the leader to help the team overcome the challenge and get everyone back on track to reach their definition of success.

How would a leader overcome it?

Let's say you have determined that a challenge exists for your team related to a team member who is not able to influence others. It may help if you look at it through the lens of the Leadership Engine of credibility, relationships, trust, and influence. If the person is struggling with influence, you could work backward and help determine the level of trust that exists. If trust is lacking, work back to relationships, and so forth. You could use your skills as a coach to help with the Leadership Engine.

The thinking behind this approach is that it helps to change your perspective when looking to overcome challenges. If you try the "How would a leader overcome it?" approach and that doesn't work, you can explore one of the other viewpoints to help force a different perspective. Keep experimenting! What matters is that you change the lens you use to look at the challenge.

Who else could or should overcome it?

This is an important decision point for you as the leader. It's possible that a challenge can be resolved directly by you, through one of any number of mechanisms.

For many people, it's rewarding to be in problem-solving mode. In fact, our brains are wired for a reward response, and solving problems can feel like a fun game.

The downside is that this leads to you becoming very tactical. When you're too tactical and hyper focused on solving problems, you can easily lose track of what you're here to do: achieve goals and deliver success.

In addition, solving problems directly may not be the best use of your time. After all, leaders are supposed to build the capabilities of others.

If it is someone else's challenge, how can I help them overcome it?

If you believe the challenge belongs to others, your role in helping to overcome it switches to that of a coach. In coach mode, you begin asking open-ended questions with the goal of helping the other person overcome their own challenge. This is especially helpful with challenges that are loaded with ambiguity.

An additional benefit of taking the coach approach is that people are often more committed to follow through on their own ideas. In highly ambiguous situations, a person's commitment level to a particular course of action may not be strong, especially if that person was told what to do by someone else. If, instead, you help them come to their own conclusion and decision, their effort level will likely be higher and their persistence and dedication will increase.

What do your values tell you?

Considering how to overcome a challenge by examining your values is another useful technique. You can use this approach to help others when they're trying to navigate an ambiguous situation or obstacle.

Having deeply rooted, explicit core values helps guide you, and others, in complex situations. Examining values can be powerful as they connect our past with the future we're seeking to create; in this way, they help us make decisions in the present.

What is my level of sensitivity and empathy to those involved?

In whatever method or approach you use to overcome the challenge, it helps if you are direct with the people involved. Remember, many of the challenges arose because of ambiguity or lack of clarity, so it's up to you to be direct, clear, and concise in your communications. While being direct is the very best way to ensure everyone knows what the challenge is and what way you are going to overcome it, it also makes a difference when you have empathy, compassion, and care during this time. Many people may have been struggling with the challenge, with high levels of frustration. You are helping them to see the challenge in a new light, with hope for resolution, and you are doing it in a direct, yet empathetic manner. This shows them that you care about them and their issues, not just about overcoming the challenge.

Your Leadership Skillset

Along with what we've shared in this module so far, this section will provide you with ideas to consider adding to your leadership skillset for dealing with challenges. Remember that, in the study of leadership, there's no single "how to" instruction manual. You get to choose what works best for you.

By going through this program, you're strengthening and enhancing a variety of competencies, as well as practicing skills, such as peer coaching and intentional stories. When you spend time in a group session working on open-ended questions, you're developing your coaching in a safe place and learning from your colleagues. As you experience the benefits of these techniques over the course of the program, you can also try to find ways to incorporate them into your processes.

Here are some familiar items to consider adding to your skillset:

- Mastermind Groups
- Intentional Story Exercises

Mastermind Groups

The principle behind a mastermind group is that tapping into the collective brainpower, wisdom, and experience of a group of people provides exponential benefits when overcoming challenges; the whole exceeds the sum of the parts.

> The idea harkens back to the early 1900s where author Napoleon Hill described Mastermind Groups as: "The coordination of knowledge and effort of two or more people, who work toward a definite purpose, in the spirit of harmony." *Think and Grow Rich. Napoleon Hill (pp 195).London, England, Penguin Group. 2003*

As with any new technique, the value and benefits derived from a mastermind group will vary based on a variety of factors. Specifically, the following factors are most likely to have a positive impact on your group:

- Having a sense of purpose for the group. What is the shared principle, topic, or reason for getting together?
- Choosing a facilitator who owns the group session. A good facilitator works hard to ensure that everyone gets a fair amount of airtime and that no one person or topic dominates the conversation.
- Striving toward accountability and success among group members.

Here are the **four most important guidelines you need to run a successful mastermind group** (or...leadership meeting, business meeting, EVERY meeting):

1. Have a specific topic for the discussion
2. Make sure the group has pertinent materials ahead of time so they come to the meeting prepared

3. Give everyone the chance to talk at every meeting. This is key to having engagement. Remember, their number one need is to be heard.

4. Make sure action items come out of every meeting. It's best if the participants choose their own action items, but it's OK if the facilitator assigns one as well.

Intentional Story Exercise

Intentional Stories are current issues or challenges (stories) that participants share during our group meeting. The storyteller embraces their vulnerability, shares a challenge they are going through (their story), and listens to open-ended questions posed by the rest of the group.

Leaders use this tool to bring clarity to otherwise ambiguous situations. If you've been a part of the Downline Leadership coaching program, you've seen the power of this exercise, how it adds value to the presenter and strengthens the coaching skills of the other participants.

Time for a story!

All I had was a hammer...

Rita had been working on the business side for about a year and had met with early success in moving up some ranks. Now, the business seemed to be slowing down a bit. She had been really happy with the tools she had been using, but wondered if the problem she was now facing was with the scripts and tools or with her? She called her upline, Natalie, to talk about her problem.

Rita: Hi Natalie! Thanks for taking a minute to chat with me.

Natalie: My pleasure, Rita. I always love when we can just plain talk. So, what's up?

Rita: As you know, I've been doing pretty well talking to prospects and then helping those that want to do the business make the transition.

Natalie: You've been doing great! So, what's going on?

Rita: Lately, the tools just haven't been working for me.

Natalie: What do you mean?

Rita: Well, the last three people who I thought for sure were going to buy kits all said no. I've replayed the conversation over in my mind, and I used the same technique I've successfully been using for the last couple of months, and I used it the exact same way with all three people, almost word for word off the script. I don't know why the same approach wouldn't work for everyone?

Natalie: Why do you think they each said no?

Rita: Each one had a different excuse.

Natalie: What observation might you make about that?

Rita: I really don't know. The same approach worked before and I don't understand why it would change? Natalie, what do you think?

Natalie (switching to mentor mode): Whenever I am faced with a problem, especially one where a process had been working and now isn't, I try to look at the feedback I receive. In your case, the feedback was unique in each case. This tells me that perhaps they needed unique solutions, not the same script. In my opinion, you use the tools to help present solutions to your customers that are individualized to them. Much of the script will apply, but it's not meant as a playbook, more as a guide. I know you see people as special and unique, you just have to marry that with your words when presenting options. (Back to coach mode) How does that sound to you?

Rita: (pause for reflection) Natalie that sounds great! I knew in the back of my mind that had to be it, but I couldn't just throw away what had been working, even when my intuition was telling me to. Makes me think of that old saying about tools, "When all you think you have is a hammer, every problem looks like a nail." Thanks Natalie!!

Discussion

Have you ever had a process go south on you? What did you do to overcome the challenge? Is it hard for you to give up on a proven process? Why?

The Path Forward

In this module, we explored the different types of challenges that a leader may encounter. We also looked at a variety of questions, approaches, and skills that can be used to determine the best path for overcoming those challenges.

Remember, it's how a leader first responds to a challenge that can make the difference in how your team will react and whether or not they will follow your lead when trying to overcome the challenge.

We'll be discussing these concepts in more detail during the group session.

Action Required

In preparation for our next group meeting, please complete the exercise on the next page.

Discussion Framework:

Use this page to capture your preliminary thoughts about this module's content. Each quadrant has questions that are provided to help stimulate your thoughts and reflections. This is not a quiz and there are no wrong answers. It's an opportunity for deep self-awareness, so capture whatever seems appropriate to you.

	INTERNAL	EXTERNAL
INDIVIDUAL	**Reflect** What did you read about this week that caught your eye and caused you to reflect? _____ _____ _____ _____ _____	**Adopt** What would you like to adopt as a going-forward behavior or process that you picked up from this week's module? _____ _____ _____ _____ _____
GROUP	**Inquire** What question would you like to ask the group concerning the topic(s) in the module? _____ _____ _____ _____ _____ _____	**Share** What insight, principle, or leadership precept did you want to share with the group? _____ _____ _____ _____ _____ _____

NOTE: *To overcome challenges will often require change. Appendix A describes a change management model. Appendix B describes one of the biggest obstacles to change... Limiting Beliefs.*

Appendix A—Method for Implementing Change to Overcome a Challenge

One of the leading resources on change management comes from John P. Kotter and his book *Leading Change.*[9] Here's a short recap on Kotter's eight-stage methodology for implementing change, which we offer as another tool in overcoming challenges. We cite here the original method, not the accelerated version:

1. **Establishing a Sense of Urgency**—Define the change in a way that will inspire people to move now! Create objectives that are real and relevant.

2. **Creating the Guiding Coalition** —Create a team of effective people who have the right commitment and the best mix of skills to implement the change.

3. **Developing a Vision and Strategy**—Cast a simple, yet powerful, vision backed up by a solid strategy to get it done.

4. **Communicating the Change Vision**—Leaders effectively communicate the nature of the vision, the changes involved, and the expected benefits. Involve as many people as possible and communicate the change in simple terms in order to appeal and respond to people's needs.

5. **Empowering Employees for Broad-Based Action**—Remove obstacles, enable constructive feedback, provide lots of support from leaders, and reward and recognize progress and achievements.

6. **Generating Short-Term Wins**—Structure the process in such a way as to have many achievable tasks and, therefore, wins when they are completed. Finish current stages before starting new ones. Celebrate the wins!

---

9   *Leading Change. pp 37-137. Cambridge, MA, Harvard Business Review Press. 2012*

7. **Consolidating Gains and Producing More Change**—Sustain the changes that have been implemented by encouraging determination and persistence throughout the change process and after. Encourage ongoing progress reporting----highlight achieved and future milestones.

8. **Anchoring New Approaches in the Culture**—Reinforce the value of successful change as it relates to success within the organization. Create a change culture.

Appendix B—Changing Limiting Beliefs to Overcome Challenges

The following model comes from author and leadership coach Julie Gutierrez and provides a potential tool for leaders who meet resistance to changes due to limiting beliefs. Keep in mind that we believe change is a foundational tool to overcome challenges, but limiting beliefs can hold those changes back. This is a summary of the Belief-to-Belief Coaching Model.

Change. Do we engage with it or are we resistant to it? If we are resistant to change, the most important question a person can ask themselves is… Why? Resistance to change often has to do with a mindset that is stuck in stone. We cannot underestimate the importance of mindsets, as they are unavoidable. What we need to understand is why we have the mindsets we have. All people have particular belief systems about their work environments, processes, systems and the relationships they interact with every day. A leader's role is to understand those beliefs as well as the perspective of circumstances an individual may have. Only then can a leader help individuals free themselves from restrictive thinking, shift their mindset to embrace empowering change and move forward to overcome challenges.

For example, one of the beliefs we've encountered in working with individuals is that change can't be enacted from the middle or be made by a single person. Using the model below, we can use open-ended questions with a person to disrupt their current thinking process. When we engage the individual in a true coaching approach, we frequently find that they begin to shift their currently held beliefs. They adjust their thinking with each step in the process to build a new belief system, thus opening the doors to new perspectives, engagement levels and advancement towards purpose.

Belief-To-Belief Coaching Model – Case Study

**Assume they say "I can't teach classes, I'm better at 1:1 coffee meetings",
this is just an example of a limiting belief.**

NOTE: In each section we've included additional questions that relate to this example of a limiting belief. For other limiting beliefs, you would change some of the words.

Process	Coaching Questions and Reflections
Belief	What does the individual currently believe? You can discover what the individual currently believes, and even why they hold this belief, through open-ended and clarifying questions such as: • What do you believe? • Why do you believe that? • Do your actions support what you say you believe? • If not, why not? What experience have you had that was negative and lead to this belief? • Do you have a belief about your personality type that limits what you believe your skills to be? • What do you know to be true about yourself that contradicts that belief? • What is the conversation that takes place in your head when you think about teaching? • What about teaching bothers you? • Under what circumstances would you consider teaching? • What is really driving your fear?
Meaning	How is the belief expressing meaning in the life of the individual? Ask questions to discover what are their day-to-day responses to situations and/or circumstances because of this belief? What do their answers reveal about the meaning they are associating with their beliefs? More questions on meaning: • When you have to teach your kids, how does that go? • What examples of teaching on a weekly basis do you have? • When you were teaching "Mary" how to use Virtual Office, how did that go? • What about larger crowds bothers you? • What skill do you think teachers have that you don't have? • Who was the best teacher you ever had? Why? • What is your definition of teaching? • What do the people in your life currently come to you for and how do you interact with them when they do? • How can you take teaching out of the box and view it from a different perspective? • How do you allow yourself to be taught and when are you your own best teacher?

Process	Coaching Questions and Reflections
Passion	The meaning that is behind the belief drives the passion of the individual. Discover how this passion is being expressed. Is it positive or negative? How does it drive their conversation? More questions on passion: • In what ways do you love to interact with others? • What other way can you reach a large number of people besides teaching? How has or could that method worked for you? • Why do you describe classes as ineffective? What are other leaders doing with their classes? • Why are you so against classes? • How long will it take you to build your business on a 1:1 basis? • How can you help yourself remove what is holding you back? • If you could have a win in this area what would it look like for you? • If you could make one small shift to give yourself more confidence what would you do? • If you had to replace the word teaching with something else to give you confidence what would you apply? How do you feel about the words, "instruct", "train", "demonstrate" or "show"?
Investment	The passion behind the belief and meaning determines the investment an individual will make. (Investment is an outward expression of an internal belief.) How does the individual you are working with "show up" in life, conversations, and interactions with others? This demonstrates their current investment. More questions on investment: • What would you be willing to do to overcome your fear? • What would it look like to you if you were an expert teacher? • No one can avoid all teaching, what can you do to become a better teacher when that is the best or only way to convey information? • What other ways of teaching can you think of? • How are you helping other leaders in your downline who are teachers? • What guidance would you give to someone in your downline who is having your same struggle? • How can you borrow confidence from another area of strength in your life to help you move forward?
People	The individual legacy that the person wants to leave is molded and impacted by the process above and causes their belief to change. More questions on people: • What if you found out you were actually good at teaching? What would you do differently with your team? • How do you want to be remembered for your teaching skills? • What would it feel like if people thought you were a great teacher? • What different impact would you have if you were a great teacher? • What have you discovered from this process that is causing you to have hope, take a risk or a step forward? • What do you now believe is possible for you and others on your team? • What is the first step forward you want to take today?

Process	Coaching Questions and Reflections
Belief	Starting with the original belief, we review our meaning, we have a renewal of passion, we make a new emotional investment, we evaluate the legacy we want to make, and we change our belief.

As we walk through the model step-by-step, we are able to see that, in order to shift a restricted or negative belief to a positive belief, one must start with identifying the roots of the current belief system. Assistance can then be given to help the individual shift meaning and develop a new, healthy passion and investment in a new belief. Offering different perspectives through which the individual can gain new hope and beliefs must be provided. This allows the individual to engage in a new process, which, in turn, affects the people around them, leaving a changed legacy, and an obstacle overcome.

Engaging in the above process opens the doors wide to self-awareness. Life can change radically when we ask ourselves the question, "What do I really believe about this and why?"

INNOVATION

In this program, we define **Innovation as *the ability to think of creative ideas and put them into action.*** It's being intentionally creative, open to new ideas, and willing to take risks. It's being unique, imaginative, different, and inspirational. Leaders care about innovation because it can accelerate the achievement of goals and bring about success.

Throughout this module, we'll look at ways that leaders relate to innovation. In addition, we'll work through what it takes to create an environment conducive to innovation for your team and downline.

Finally, we'll look at a variety of practical things you can do to support and encourage the use of innovation in your business.

Module Overview

In experiencing this module you will:

- Consider the different ways that innovation relates to Downline Leadership and how innovation actually happens.

- Examine the significance of supporting and promoting innovation in your business and learn how to move from creativity to implementation.

- Learn how to activate creativity in your business.

What is Innovation?

> *"Innovation and leadership are closely related. Leadership always has some focus on bringing about a better future. In this sense, leaders are necessarily innovators."*
>
> –Jim Selman
>
> *Leadership, pg 39, Pearson Education do Brasil. 2009*

Innovation involves creating new ideas, process changes, or solutions that, when executed, propel your team and business forward. Implementation of creativity is taking ideas, turning them into reality, AND delivering a higher level of value. It's not just about having good (or great) ideas; it's about executing those ideas for the benefit of your business, your customer, and your team.

A key element of innovation is that it's done *through* people. That's why it takes a leader to lead a team through innovation. People generate the ideas, people implement the ideas, and *people* are what leaders do best! One of your best tools for innovation is your intuition; understanding their comfort level, their trust level, and their commitment and willingness to be creative, can make the innovation session more effective.

Innovation matters to leaders because, in a rapidly changing and complex world full of challenges, **innovation trumps planning**. Planning assumes that what worked before will work again; **innovation understands that making sense of new situations requires new competencies**. Let's look at how creativity and innovation are tied at the hip.

Creativity

Creativity is the ability to transcend traditional thinking, rules, and patterns by creating new interpretations, methods, or practices. Some call this *ideation*.

The challenge for many of us is that we're used to traditional thinking, adhering to rules, and predictable patterns. Why? Because it's worked. Everything with a process or a methodology was created with a primary purpose: to increase repeatability. Repeatability and predictability are at the opposite end of the spectrum from creativity.

Note: we're not making any judgments about the importance of any of these attributes; what's important is recognizing that there's a time and a place for them. The important thing for a leader is to find the right balance between repeatability and creativity.

When you focus on creativity, you are enabling one of the most crucial factors for future success. As the marketplace continues to grow more volatile, complex, and responsive to shifting customer demand, top performing people need creative thinking more than rigor and disciplined management. We need only reflect on how social media has changed network marketing to see the impact of creativity. What new idea will change the world next?

When do you need Innovation?

As you explore this module, you should find much that is relevant to situations you face day-in and day-out. Here is a partial list of situations where innovation could hold the key to success:

In a relationship

Suppose you have a relationship that has stalled. Innovation can possibly break the stalemate. Introducing new ideas to the way you connect can get the relationship moving forward. Sometimes it's as simple as communicating using a different format. Sometimes it is harder and the innovation has to be more creative. It may not be enough to send a text to break the logjam; maybe you have to talk with them, listen well, and then move the discussion in *their* direction.

What if you can't get a relationship started? Sometimes, you have someone who simply won't engage with you, and you don't know them well enough to come up with some creative idea to connect with them. In this situation, the innovative approach may be the direct one. Call them. This may sound simple, but in today's social media world, calling someone has become an innovative approach.

To overcome a challenge

Innovation is one approach you can use to attack a challenge. You may face a challenge for which there isn't already a viable solution that fits in terms of having been proven effective and efficient. To get through this type of challenge, having the right attitude is key. If you can convey excitement, curiosity, and a "we can do it" mindset, you can inspire the team to see this challenge in a new light and activate their creativity.

When you have a "routine" process or a sacred cow

The process that seems to have the least opportunity for innovation may actually be the best playground for innovative thoughts.

Routine processes are those that have been done over and over, or for which an established, repeatable methodology exists. Subjecting a routine process to an innovation-oriented exercise will gain one of two benefits: you'll either determine if a better alternative exists or you'll be more confident that the routine approach really is the best one.

For example, suppose your team follows a strict process for making customer care calls. Feedback from those customers has identified a need for change. Time for innovation.

In a similar vein, "untouchables" are processes, topics, or ideas that are considered exempt from criticism or questioning. Anytime you hear "that's how we always do it," it should be a red flag for a leader to consider what could happen if innovation collided with tradition.

Event Planning

Let's say you're planning a new event that you and your team have never held before. As the leader, you have an opportunity to help shape and influence aspects of the event.

Due to high levels of credibility and a strong leadership legacy from your prior events, you're able to facilitate brainstorming sessions where a multitude of ideas are generated on how to organize and run the new event. This is a tremendous opportunity to help foster the activation of creativity.

Having the ability to facilitate and bring value to these event planning discussions is a significant step toward helping shape and influence event success. As you proceed in this direction, you increase the likelihood that you'll be able to encourage creativity once the event planning gets underway.

Now that we've looked at different scenarios in which you may want innovation, let's go deeper by exploring how to actually activate creativity.

Activation of Creativity

How leaders **activate** creativity and foster the formation of ideas is important, because innovation can require a different mindset than the one with which most people are comfortable. The reason is that we all have biases; we've reached a position and point in our lives where certain thought patterns and routines have served us well.

Our success to date is partially due to our ability to call upon prior patterns of thought that have worked well and to reuse them. The better you are at one particular way of thinking, the harder it can be to see things another way.

> "There is nothing in a caterpillar that tells you it's going to be a butterfly."
> —R. Buckminster Fuller
>
> US engineer and architect, 1895-1983

When an idea is introduced that's contradictory to these established patterns, it can be difficult to objectively assess its worth.

Activation is finding a way to allow these new ideas and thoughts to come forth. Leaders have to take action and innovate; the futures of their businesses may depend on it.

For you, it will require revisiting your level of self-awareness and exploring your own thought process about innovation. Then, when you're creating a safe environment for others to innovate in, you can observe whether they, too, are opening up their thought processes or if you need to help them find ways to remove obstacles to innovation.

Now that we've established the importance of activating creativity, let's get into more specifics on the leader's role in innovation.

Role of the Leader

Leaders have two responsibilities that relate to Innovation:

- Internal: how do you as the leader use innovation to achieve your goals?

- External: how do you create an environment for your team that is conducive to innovation?

Internal

The leader can use innovation in several different ways to reach their own goals. The leader mindset for innovation might include a willingness to make frequent mistakes, have false starts, or take wrong turns. From failures and mistakes come learning and the potential for improvement (see final section in this module "What if Innovation Fails")!

> "There are risks and costs to action. But they are far less than the long-range risks of comfortable inaction."
>
> –John F. Kennedy
>
> US President 1960-1962

As we'll see shortly, when in "Innovation Mode," the behaviors are counterintuitive for many of us.

Here are some other traits a leader needs to be innovative:

- **Curiosity**—This is a hallmark characteristic of innovators. Having your mind set in a neutral place, with no judgmental thoughts, is a baseline requirement of curiosity. This place of genuine inquisitiveness yields a series of questions that lead to insight and increased awareness. The questions that come from a truly curious mind can provide interesting opportunities for innovation.

- **Courage**—Perhaps one of the most important ingredients for innovation is courage. The innovative leader must be willing to take risks, rattle some cages, and move forward without the fear of failure. They must see change as an ally in their war to achieve value for the customer, and they must be ready and willing to take action. This doesn't mean that they don't do their homework to analyze their creative solution and its impact; it just means that, in the end, they can take the risk, pull the trigger, and implement the idea.

- **Tolerance for ambiguity**—The complex nature of today's consumer markets, coupled with a need for fast-paced decision-making, means that leaders often operate in highly ambiguous environments. In times of ambiguity, the leader will need to stick to their convictions, retain their integrity, not get frustrated or lost, and use innovation to bring clarity to their situation.

- **Balance and Agility**—Leaders need to allow for the ebb and flow of the marketplace to drive innovation. There's a time for *activation* of creativity and there's a time for *implementation.* Having balance between these two forces is a key competency for leaders. While balance is critical, leaders also need to see the value of being agile and implementing innovative ideas quickly.

- **Intuition**—Leaders listen to what is said and to what is *not* said. They gather data from all angles, including their gut. They sense when someone on the team is onto something new and innovative and when they're not. They mix the hard data with the soft data and craft a vision that includes innovative ideas.

External

The leader is responsible for creating a culture conducive to innovation for their team and downline. In this capacity, the leader may need to foster collaborative team meetings. Here are some thoughts on how to support that.

Foster collaborative team meetings that are focused on creativity. Leaders inspire innovation by stimulating discussion and reflection among the team in a safe environment. This requires trust and the establishment of some of the same mindset requirements discussed above (e.g. curiosity) in the members of the team. Innovation is difficult for many because we're not used to airing our new and out-of-the-box ideas in public. This requires vulnerability and safety, which is the environment leaders need to create. Asking open-ended questions is a great way to foster an environment of creativity.

Recognize and remove barriers to innovation. Over time, some teams have created a culture that's a barrier to innovation. Compliance is rewarded and innovation is discouraged. Leaders in these environments need to create a safe and trusting place for members to try out new ideas.

One of the fundamental things a leader can do is to set expectations for meetings where you expect an innovative mindset.

Establish Ground Rules for Innovation Meetings

- Assume everyone is there to collaborate and be creative.
- Find value in the ideas.
- Recognize and build on ideas.
- Suspend judgment regarding one's own & others' ideas.
- Share the airtime.

Here are two methodologies, brainstorming and improvisation, which you can use for conducting an innovation meeting. There are others (SCAMMPERR, Lateral Thinking, Mind Mapping, Fishbone Diagram, Problem Reversal, Attribute Listing), but these first two are the most common and engaging ways to have an innovation meeting:

Brainstorming (originated by Alex F. Osborn, 1888-1966)

1. Organize a group of four to eight participants (ideally).
2. Choose the topic (problem) and write it on a board (virtual or physical). Make sure everyone understands the problem.
3. Establish ground rules:
   a. Do not criticize. All ideas are welcome and valid. This ensures that everyone and their ideas are valued.

    b. Do not limit the number of ideas. The goal of brainstorming is to get a large number of ideas.

    c. Do not filter or censor any ideas. Keep the brainstorming session flowing.

    d. Listen to the ideas and use them to generate more ideas.

    e. Do not discuss the idea as this could stop the flow.

    f. Have no restrictions on time, money, or resources. Sometimes even outrageous ideas can help the team get out of the box, stretch their thinking, and come up with new ideas.

4. The facilitator can conduct the session either in an unstructured way (any person in the group can give ideas at any time) or structured (going around the group for ideas).

5. The facilitator must be engaged to enforce the rules and write down all ideas. The facilitator needs to also be attentive to how the team is responding and reacting to ensure that the environment continues to be safe, trusting, and creative.

6. The facilitator should clarify and conclude the session.

7. The facilitator should obtain a consensus on how the group wants to move forward and implement.

Improvisation (Improv)

Commonly thought of as a comedic technique, Improv is rapidly becoming a powerful creativity-stimulating technique that can be used to produce significant results. The power of Improv is that it teaches participants how to be mindful, how to react and adapt quickly to changing circumstances, and how to communicate effectively.

To newcomers, Improv may seem unstructured and random, yet there are actually guidelines that create a structure that governs what happens. Google "Improv exercises" for additional ideas that you can run with your team, but here are a few examples to get you started:

- **Accept all offers.** Offers are statements, ideas, or concepts that are put forth by others. Improv starts with an offer. For example, saying to another person, "I am going to make an apple pie by using an apple," when your hands are empty, but shaped as if you were holding an apple, is an offer. The other person then accepts that offer by continuing the discussion as if, in fact, they were now holding an apple. You keep going around the group and accepting what is given to you and creating new ways to use apples and make pies. Now try this idea using a network marketing scenario like, "I am holding my first 101 class at the local library" and have the rest of the team explore what that might look like.

- **Agree and say "Yes, and..."** No matter how outlandish the offer, the exchange with the other person continues with a "Yes, and..." mindset. Using the example above, the other person might respond with "Yes, and that apple can be infused with orange juice." The two people then keep coming up with new additions to the story. Keeping the network marketing idea going... "Yes, and I've heard that the library staff is very supportive of groups meeting there."

- **Add to the conversation, without asking questions.** Each improv is built by people, one statement at a time. As the conversation passes back and forth between the participants, new information is added that takes things in interesting and different directions. For example: Mary says, "I tried a new pie yesterday." June says, "Where each fruit was put in a blender." Kyla says, "And infused with different juices," and Mary closes with, "That shows how many different ways there are to make a pie." Take one idea and keep adding to it. Questions don't add new information; instead, they add more work for other participants. One more time for network marketing... "I held my class at the library", "Where the environment kept their focus", "And each person really listened to the presentation", "Which shows we can have 101 classes anywhere!".

The use of improv as part of a creativity-generating meeting can build trust, increase collaboration and communication, and help participants feel more self-confident and less afraid to make mistakes. Now try to visualize an Improv with your team using a real problem like the one about holding a class in the library above.

What happens when a leader is able to do these things? People understand that their ideas have merit, and they trust that it's safe to express those ideas. Furthermore, they're more likely to be successful at implementing those ideas because they're more committed to them.

Transition from Activation to Implementation

Activating creativity isn't sufficient for innovation; innovation requires implementation as well. The implementation of creativity may not be as exciting, fun, or creative as generating the ideas themselves, but it's extremely important. Implementation is what turns good and great ideas into true business value.

At some point, the leader has to shift the mindset and culture from safe, encouraging, and open (which allows for idea generation) to specific, focused, and execution-minded.

Properly handling this transition is key, because the goodwill and trust that have been established during activation needs to be maintained for effective implementation.

Furthermore, maintaining the level of engagement and buy-in of those who participated in the activation is critical since these participants are typically the same people who will be called upon to help drive implementation.

During the transition time, you have to be tuned into the attitudes and mindset of the team. Inevitably, some ideas will not make the cut, and the people who were the sponsors of those ideas may not be fully committed to the implementation of the ideas that *do* make the cut. Maintaining strong relationships and commitments to the goals is critical at this point.

It is also important to cultivate an environment where there's no fear of failure. The leader and the team have to be ready to take risks to move the ideas through implementation.

Implementation

The *implementation* of creativity is where a leader can really make their mark. Here are four key points to consider during implementation.

- **Make sure the ideas are connected to your goals.** It may be a great idea, it might be desirable for the customer, but it may also be unrelated to your goals. You need to determine if this is the right time or place for this particular innovation.

- **Ensure ongoing engagement.** If you are fully engaged during the activation process, they're more likely to buy into the implementation phase.

- **Own the innovation.** As the owner of your business, you need to own the innovation and the changes it brings. This isn't just an exercise in coming up with new ideas; it's about developing new ways to move forward and successfully executing those new plans. You own the process of facilitating the *creation* of the ideas, *executing* the ideas, and *marketing* and *championing* the ideas to your team and downline.

- **Evolve and grow your use of innovation:**
  1. Use someone else's idea and someone else's method to implement the idea.
  2. Use someone else's idea and YOUR OWN method to implement the idea.
  3. Use YOUR OWN idea and YOUR OWN method to implement the idea.

Finally, ask yourself these questions to ensure you've implemented something worthwhile:

- Have you disrupted the status quo and delivered something of genuine value to the customer or the team?
- Did you take advantage of current trends to truly innovate?
- Did you leverage what you already had in place to create new opportunities?
- What customer needs have NOT yet been met?

What if Innovation Fails?

When you find yourself unable to be creative or put new ideas into action, you will have to do some troubleshooting.

We have no new ideas!

Remember when we said EVERYONE has intuition. The same is true with creativity. If everyone has it, then why can't you and your team come up with new ideas?

- Look internally first. How are you modeling creativity? When was the last time you came up with a new idea?

- Look at your environment next. How creative are your internal brainstorming sessions? How creative was your last team brainstorming sessions? Here are some questions to reflect on: Did you shut down the furthest-reaching ideas? Did you let the newer members of the team share their ideas? When the last idea failed, did you get upset with yourself, or worse, with the team? Why do you expect the team to want to try new ideas?

None of our ideas work!

"We have great ideas, but each time we try to put them into action, they don't work."

- What level of planning did you do to make sure the right resources were in place to ensure success?

- How was the team involved in taking their idea all the way to fruition?

- How did the team own the idea?

- What is the culture around failure and learning from mistakes?

In reality, you can't have innovation without mistakes and failure. You, as the Leader, must have empathy for those going through failure, especially if it's you that had the failed idea. Help them to get back to the drawing board and begin coming up with new ideas. Conduct a review of the effort, find out what you and the team can learn from the failure, and put that valuable information to use on the next idea, because it's going to be great!

> "Only one factor separates those who consistently achieve from those who do not. The difference between average people and achieving people is their perception of and response to failure."
>
> –John Maxwell
>
> *Failing Forward, pg 2, Thomas Nelson, Nashville, TN. 2000*

But, it's the best idea!

Jean was getting ready for the brainstorming meeting. She was quite excited, as the team had been planning for two weeks and she knew they had a lot of ideas. As long as those ideas supported her strategy, she was going to be very happy!

Jean: Thank you for coming tonight and sharing your ideas on how we can provide a better way for new members to get on board. There are eight of us, so instead of going around in a circle, let's take ideas as you want to present them, OK?

(Team nods in acceptance)

Madison: I'd like to suggest that we customize our approach so that each new member feels really welcomed.

Jean: Thanks Madison, great suggestion! Who'd like to go next?

Kloey: What if we made a personal call to each new member? That would make them feel special.

Jean: Another wonderful suggestion! Let's keep these ideas rolling!

Emma: Another way we can make it unique to the new member is if we give them a list of welcome gifts they can choose from. They would get what they wanted, and we'd get a chance to learn a little bit more about them.

Jean: Emma, this idea is super! Wow, you guys sure have given this some thought, and these ideas are so creative! I'd like to suggest an idea that I think each of you will like. Here's my strategy. Let's work together to create a really nice welcome card and combine it with a gift. By giving everyone the same card and gift, we'll treat everyone the same and no one will feel hurt. With just one type of gift, we can make sure that we always have enough, and we'll know what it will cost to ship. So, what does everyone think of my idea?

The team looks at each other, discouraged, but not really wanting to fight for their ideas involving customization. So, they acquiesce and agree to Jean's idea.

Three months later, the team got together to discuss the results of their new member welcome process. It turned out that Jean was right about cost and shipping, and no one had complained about being mistreated. However, the vast majority of new members just threw away the card and gift, and no one really cared. Was this really "our" best idea?

Discussion

What do you think of Jean's handling of the meeting? What type of innovation environment do you think she created? What do you think Jean heard when the team was trying to go after a custom solution? Would you have done anything differently? What would you do now after hearing the results of the last three months?

The Path Forward

In this module we explored different scenarios under which innovation could be a relevant and useful approach to achieving your goals.

The module covered what it means to create an environment/culture of creativity for you and your team. This approach leads to generating new ideas for how to improve overall business.

We also looked at the difference between the activation of creativity and the implementation of it, with particular emphasis on the transition from one to the other.

We'll be discussing these concepts in more detail during the group session.

Action Required

In preparation for our next group meeting, please complete the exercise on the next page.

Discussion Framework:

Use this page to capture your preliminary thoughts about this module's content. Each quadrant has questions that are provided to help stimulate your thoughts and reflections. This is not a quiz and there are no wrong answers. It's an opportunity to deepen self-awareness, so capture whatever seems appropriate to you.

	INTERNAL	EXTERNAL
INDIVIDUAL	**Reflect** What did you read about this week that caught your eye and caused you to reflect? _Innovation Requires Creativity & put Into action_	**Adopt** What would you like to adopt as a going-forward behavior or process that you picked up from this week's module? _① plan better - Right Resources for better success_ _② I like to jump In before planning_
GROUP	**Inquire** What question would you like to ask the group concerning the topic(s) in the module?	**Share** What insight, principle, or leadership precept did you want to share with the group?

BALANCE AND AGILITY

Competing and conflicting priorities constantly barrage downline leaders. This module focuses on helping you learn to balance those challenges, along with helping you to identify what type of agility it takes to achieve that balance.

Each of your businesses is different because each customer, each team, and each leader is unique. What worked yesterday may not work tomorrow. What *does* work is balancing the different needs of your business while being nimble and responsive to the constantly changing world we live in.

This module will bring more awareness to the role that balance and agility play in your development as a leader. As you grow in this skill set, you'll be able to navigate competing interests and find balance amidst the chaos.

Module Overview

In completing this module you will:

- Appreciate the balance and agility requirements of your business, your customer, and your team.

- Explore how to shift the fulcrum to achieve balance.

- Determine when it's appropriate to adopt the role of director, teacher, mentor, or coach.

What is Balance and Agility?

Leaders show their **balance** by being *stable* and *at peace* with the conflicting needs of their businesses, teams, and families. When life hits you from all sides and throws you out of balance, leaders show their **agility** by being *nimble* and *responsive* to those different needs and by being able to get back in balance.

Almost every decision a leader makes involves balancing conflicting needs. Do I go fast or slow? Do I speak or do I listen? Do we stick to the plan or do we innovate? Leaders find the balance between these and other contrasting interests.

When you are making balance decisions, you will find that you need to be agile, as the balance you strive for can shift quickly. There are so many different types of people and circumstances that even when you reach a place of balance, that balance is short-lived. But, that's OK! A leader's agility enables them to continually adjust their role, their focus, or their intention in order to regain their balance. Balance and agility go hand in hand.

Why are balance and agility critical to a leader? They're important because, not only is each business different, but each day *in the same business* is also different. As the ancient Greek philosopher Heraclitus put it, "You cannot step in the same river twice." Most people understand that a river is dynamic and fluid; the hidden meaning in this statement is revealed when the emphasis is on the word "you." You also change each day and are a different person today than you were yesterday. Not only are you different daily, so are the people you're leading. As a result, continually adjusting for balance is critical to your effectiveness as a leader, and you can't do that without also being agile.

> *"Yesterday's leadership theories are not keeping pace with the velocity of today's disruptive marketplace. Organizations are seeking a new model for the age of agility."*
> –Bill Pelster
>
> *Leadership Next: Debunking the superhero myth. From the "2013 Human Capital Trends" published by Deloitte.*

Let's explore the fundamentals of balance and agility in more depth.

Balance

For our purposes, *balance* is achieved when competing forces exist in proper proportion to each other and one does not outweigh the other. It also means that a state of equilibrium exists. However, keep in mind that balance doesn't necessarily mean that the components are present in a 50:50 split.

Here are some ways that balance is manifested in the context of Downline Leadership:

- Balance between work and family

- Balance between when to be a manager and when to be a leader

- Balance within the Downline Leadership competencies

Balance between work and family

Perhaps the most common out-of-balance situation we hear of is when leaders work too many hours or work at the wrong time, thereby negatively impacting their families. So many people's "why" concerns their family, yet they frequently focus more on their business than on spending time with their family. And when you become a major contributor (or primary) financial provider for the family, the pressure to work harder mounts even further. You have to find balance!

Finding balance in the middle of constant change is challenging and often, downright impossible! You've got an event at the school, a doctor's visit, and an online business event, all at the same time. Your spouse is doing everything they can, but it's not enough. As bad as that example sounds, there are many of you saying that, compared to most of your days, that day would be a walk in the park. The result is that your family suffers as you try to find balance.

How many times have you heard, "You listen better to your customers than you do to me!" or, "You care more about your team's families than you do about ours!" As much as you care about your customers, it pales in comparison to how much you really care about your own family. So, how is it possible that your family believes the opposite? Lack of balance. You're not balancing the time you spend, the focus you exert, and the presence you have. You're just not there when your family really needs you.

This isn't easy for you. Your business frequently represents your passion, and some of your family responsibilities represent pure drudgery. Don't tell me you're *eager* to do the laundry! What does your family see at this point? They see your excitement level rise when you're talking about your business, and they see your energy level going down when you have to take one of the kids to the dentist.

Lastly, there is the problematic *help* issue. Your family sees you go out of your way to help your teammates but feels you won't bend your schedule to give them more time. You're frequently seen being the most helpful person on the planet, outside of the house. This isn't the real you, but it's the one your family sees.

It's critical that leaders stay in tune with the needs of their families, and that when it's time to stop working, they stop for the sake of their families. Conversely, if working is unavoidable (as it sometimes is), it's suggested that leaders proactively communicate with their families and do what they can ahead of time to support their family's needs during the time that they'll be unavailable. Focus on *saying* you love them and *showing* them that you do, as often as you can. Here are a couple of tips:

- Set expectations with your family about your daily calendar.
- Be mindful of your own office hours. This is WORK time.
- Establish rules for interruptions.
- Don't miss opportunities to connect.

Why did we write so much on this particular balance issue? Being out of balance with your family can be a deal breaker. You'll also want to pay close attention to the section coming up on "How Do You Achieve Balance?"

Balance between being a manager and being a leader

Another out-of-balance issue is deciding when to manage versus when to lead. To achieve business success, leadership does not replace management; they coexist. Management is concerned with the tactical and critical elements of your business—orders, schedules, resources, and budgets. On the other hand, leadership is focused on leading the team and customer to optimal success. Both have to be accomplished with excellence. You are simultaneously a manager and a leader. The effective leader achieves that delicate balance when they know which role to emphasize to achieve maximum impact.

Balance within leadership competencies

Balance is a very important theme that's discussed within many of our competency modules. See below for a summary:

Module	How Balance Matters
Downline Leadership	When you're defining success with your team, it's a delicate balancing act. Balancing the needs for growth, prosperity, fulfillment, impact, and health requires a leader.
Innovation	There's a constant battle between creativity and implementation. You shouldn't just think of new ideas, and then implement none of them. Nor should you just do business as usual without being innovative. Either of these approaches would result in a lack of balance in your business.
Leaving a Legacy	Leaders understand the long-term implications of each interaction with another person. Finding balance with people on an ongoing basis creates a leadership legacy.

Module	How Balance Matters
Leadership Engine	Since relationships are about connecting with others, the leader has to find that balance in how others want to be approached, listened to, and related to.
Ownership and Accountability	Leaders strive to own their business but have to be careful they don't begin to own their teammates' businesses. Finding balance between holding on and letting go will define your leadership and ownership.
Communication	Find your balance between the time you spend speaking to others and the time you spend listening to them.
Intuition	An effective leader balances his or her emotions with their intuition, never letting either get out of hand.

How Do You Achieve Balance?

What's the secret to achieving balance? Move the fulcrum! We've all seen teeter-totters in action. When someone large is seated across from someone small, the smaller person is stuck up in the air. However, when the fulcrum is moved closer to the larger person, balance is immediately restored between the two.

This same principle works for balancing challenges within your business. Find which issue the fulcrum needs to be closer to, and you'll attain balance. Said another way, find where you need to place your effort, then focus and move that way. This will move the fulcrum and help create balance. For example, say that you are meeting with your team and trying to decide whether to hold a training class for new business people or an introduction to the product line for potential new customers. There is no right or wrong answer. Ask open-ended questions to uncover which the team feels is the greater need. If that need is to help new business people, then use your influence with the team to shift the discussion and utilization of resources toward that option. Move the fulcrum closer to the training class.

Now, be careful that you don't move the fulcrum too far. The leader's world is constantly changing, so where the fulcrum rests constantly changes as well. Balance is the goal. It's a fleeting position, but keep working at it and you'll find yourself able to quickly and deftly find the new resting spot for your focus.

Let's take a different look at what it means to be in balance. Instead of the teeter-totter, close your eyes and visualize the person performing at a street fair that has a bunch of plates spinning on the top of sticks. How does he keep all of the plates going and not falling? Balance! How do *you* achieve that balance? Skill, training, experience, and, most importantly, prioritization.

Think about it—the street performer loves to show you how to keep three plates, then four plates, then six plates all spinning. Yet, he doesn't do a hundred plates, does he? It's the same for you. You have to choose which plates to keep spinning. No one, absolutely no one, can keep all the plates spinning, all of the time. You have to prioritize which plates are the most important to you. The best way to do this is to reflect back on your values and on your "why." Use your intuition to know which plate needs to stay spinning no matter what. Go back a few paragraphs and remember our conversation about your family. Schedule your time based on your *"why"* and your goals. Invest your time in the most important things, and you'll keep those plates spinning. This is easy to understand, but very hard to do every day.

A hallmark of leadership is mastering tradeoff decisions between what's urgent and what's important, and recognizing that those two are not always the same. Use the four-quadrant model below to evaluate your time/energy. You'll see the four D's in the parenthesis.

	Not Important	Important
Not Urgent	Don't do (Dump it)	Wait (Delay it)
Urgent	Have someone else do it (Delegate it)	GOLD (Dig in)

Let's close the discussion of balance by listing some other typical dichotomies a leader has to deal with. What are some of yours?

- Lead from in front vs. lead from behind
- Stay the course vs. change direction
- Introduce small changes vs. introduce large changes
- Make the decision on your own vs. make the decision as a team
- Take a risk vs. keep the ship stable
- Focus on the future vs. focus on the present
- Plan for growth vs. plan for sustainability

As we disclosed earlier, the way to achieve balance is to be agile. Let's dig into what agility looks like.

Agility

Agility is the ability to move and shift your focus to maintain balance and includes several different attributes: adaptability, proportionality, nimbleness, and flexibility.

Adaptability

In your business, you'll need to adapt your style based on what's happening as well as on what needs to happen. For example, there will be times where you need to cultivate an open environment where creativity, innovation, and freethinking can occur in a safe place. At other times, you may enter a critical phase where a decision has to be made. At that point, adapting to the needs of the business means locking things down and making the decision.

Proportionality

Proportionality means putting in an amount of effort and action that corresponds to the size of the task. The greater the importance of a task, the greater the investment of time and resources that is required. Proportionality also applies to how fast you change. Again, as the task increases in importance, you must be prepared to increase the speed with which you move to meet the changing need.

Nimbleness

Managers are already nimble at handling the typical changes, issues, and other course corrections that occur in a business. For you as the leader, however, nimbleness is about navigating the gray zones that can occur when working with different people. People can have competing interests or conflicting personalities. Either way, the leader must adroitly handle those kinds of conversations and interactions to be effective.

Flexibility

A flexible leader learns quickly and applies those lessons in an effective manner. Flexible leaders are open to new ideas and are able to think and draw conclusions in a speedy manner. Agile and flexible leaders are situational leaders.

Agility is in effect when leaders vary their roles between coach, mentor, teacher, and director based on the needs of the situation. We call this ability to switch hats on a moment's notice *Role Agility*. We covered this originally in the Coaching module and we'll review it again later in the next section.

Another example of being flexible is when you need to shift between a manager mindset and a leader mindset. This adjustment may occur not just day-to-day, but often several times hourly! Each interaction you have with another person requires you to be agile and balanced in how you approach that interaction.

Let's look at role agility in greater depth.

Role Agility

One of the ways agility manifests is through your adaptability in your role. For example, we previously explored the concept of how being a leader coexists with being a manager. Other hats a leader may wear from time-to-time include that of director, teacher, mentor, or coach.

A leader doesn't have the luxury of one leadership style. Because everyone on the team is different, it takes balancing multiple leadership styles and the agility to flow between them to effectively reach the team.

A neutral approach to these roles is best, combined with a coach-first approach of asking questions to assess which role is needed. There are times when the speed of decision-making indicates the need to be a director; other times you'll need to be more of a coach. Also, it's very important that you are transparent when switching roles. Your audience sees your actions, and trust strengthens when they understand why you are doing what you are doing.

The other influencing factor is your intuition. You need to use your intuition to determine which role is best for the situation. You also need to factor in your strengths. It's usually best to lead from your area of strength. Let's say that your strongest role is that of teacher. While we still recommend using a coach-first approach to any situation to learn what's going on, we realize that you're going to be at your best when teaching. So, gather the data you need to do a great job of teaching, while leaving yourself open to the other roles when your intuition tells you to shift.

Let's look more specifically at how agility is applied in the specific roles we fill as leaders.

Director (You tell others)

Many of us have this one down. When time is short, when action is required, when the team is stuck, taking the director role is appropriate. Remember though, that this role is the least relational one and should be used the least. This role has the nature of a *push* —you push the team.

Teacher (You show others)

The teacher role involves more interaction, more giving on your part. However, it's still a push: you to them. As such, the relational element is lacking in this role as well. When you have information or ways to do things and your audience does not, adopting the teacher role is the best way to get this information to them.

Mentor (You share with others)

More relational than teaching is being a mentor. The other person is seeking your opinion. It's actually quite an honor, as they really want to hear what you have to say. However, don't lose sight of the other person. No matter what you say, they still have to figure out how to use what you share with them in their own business. Their business is different from yours, and they will apply your words of wisdom in a different way than you have. That's OK! Try to listen more when you ask what they're going to do with the information you've shared with them. This will help deepen your relationship with them.

Coach (You ask others)

This role involves the highest level of relationship and can be the most powerful of all the roles as the purpose of the coach is to empower the other person. Using open-ended questions, you're able to help others figure out their own path.

Coach-first means seeking first to understand. We highly recommend that you ask questions first, then balance the answers you receive with your intuition to determine which role to take.

You may recall that we spent an entire module, "Coaching," on this role because it's *that* important to the leader.

Balancing Your Message

Mary had been struggling with her latest Facebook posts in her business group. Her theme was straightforward, "Share your favorite oil story." Her post had been seen by over fifty people, yet only two people had commented. So, she posted again...and, then again...and, then again.

Jill, one of Mary's level one leaders, saw all of the posts and gave Mary a call.

Jill: Mary, how are you doing?

Mary: Jill, to be honest, I'm beside myself. I've written a post about sharing oil stories four times now. Each time, I make the post a little different, and no one is responding to any of them!

Jill: Why do you think that everyone is being quiet?

Mary: I have no idea! I keep asking them to post a comment, but they keep ignoring me.

Jill: What kind of style do you think your writing is in?

Mary: Well, the first one was really open and engaging, but the later ones... they kind of got a little more direct. {Sigh} Do you think they're not responding because I got too pushy?

Jill: Why don't you reread your posts right now and let me know what you think. Put yourself in the shoes of one of your busy business people. What do you read?

{Pause while Mary reads the four posts.}

Mary: Jill, I'm kind of embarrassed. These posts get more direct and downright pushy with each one. By the last one, it almost reads like I'm yelling at them to comment. I can't believe I wrote them. Where was my head?

Jill: Don't be so hard on yourself, Mary. You obviously care a great deal about the oils and desire strongly to help people share their story. What do you think you lost sight of?

Mary: I lost my balance in my message. Instead of letting the first post speak for itself, I started to get mad and started to demand comments. I should have given people more time to answer the first one, letting the post hang out there for a while. Maybe I could have called some people to have them comment and even commented myself, sharing my own story. Finding balance sure can be hard!

Jill: I think you just found it☺

Discussion

What do you think of Jill's agility in shifting between coach, teacher, mentor, and director roles? Was she effective? What would you have done if you were in Jill's shoes?

The Path Forward

In this module we explored what it takes for leaders to achieve balance and agility.

Balance is critical to success and can be difficult to obtain. One of the ways leaders find balance is by moving the fulcrum. Leaders use their intuition to decide which things to focus on to reach optimal balance, hence moving the fulcrum.

In addition, we reviewed the additional roles a leader could take depending on the needs of the business.

In the end, leaders seek to deliver success through the path that delivers the greatest value to their customers and their team. Balance and agility are enablers of that path.

Action Required

In preparation for our next group meeting, please complete the exercise on the next page.

wk end
work out an
& an
- family

week
5-6 workout
8-5 shop
6 - 8 YL fac
8 - 10 Scott

Discussion Framework:

Use this page to capture your preliminary thoughts about this module's content. Each quadrant has questions that are provided to help stimulate your thoughts and reflections. This is not a quiz and there are no wrong answers. It's an opportunity to deepen self-awareness, so capture whatever seems appropriate to you.

	INTERNAL	**EXTERNAL**
INDIVIDUAL	**Reflect** What did you read about this week that caught your eye and caused you to reflect? can't step in same River twice Dump - Delay - delegate - Do it game Planner ⭐	**Adopt** What would you like to adopt as a going-forward behavior or process that you picked up from this week's module? { Working hours from 6 - 8pm Work hard & efficient & fast as I can Balance why ← Schedule 3x5 card write why done tear up
GROUP	**Inquire** What question would you like to ask the group concerning the topic(s) in the module? ⭐ win the day - 3-5 things that must be done — win the day ● eddie ● Bullet Journal	**Share** What insight, principle, or leadership precept did you want to share with the group? greater the Importance the greater the Involvement & task

My priorties ▪️Schedule
why ➚ - plan
① kids -
family
② bi 2 YL
③ Health
④ shop
⑤ Husband

LEAVING A LEGACY

Legacy is the lasting contribution and impact you leave with others. It's what you're known for, and it's how others remember you. Legacy is created through helping others achieve more than they could have by themselves. It's achieved as you lead the team to attain their goals and deliver value to their customers. It's realized with the experience everyone went through to get it done together.

As we approach the end of this program, it's time to explore the leadership legacy you're leaving behind. Remember the fundamental questions we asked at the beginning of the book:

Do I see myself as a leader?

Do others see me as a leader?

Well… do they? There are no accidental leaders; being a leader takes ownership and intentionality. You have to *choose* to be a leader. In much the same way, leaders are intentional about their legacy. They *think* about their legacy and are focused on forming one that is powerful, influential and lasting.

By thinking about their legacy, leaders create leadership equity for the future. That's when others see you as a leader!

Module Overview

In experiencing this module you will:

- Consider the nature of a leadership legacy and why it's important to build your legacy today.

- Examine different ways in which your legacy is left and how it impacts others.

- Explore how your legacy could last forever.

- Determine how leaving a legacy integrates with other Downline Leadership competencies.

What Does It Mean To Leave A Legacy?

Just a moment ago, we defined your legacy as the lasting contribution and impact you leave with others. Let's examine each of the definition components in more detail.

The lasting contribution...

The lasting contribution is a result of the ongoing investment you've made in other people while you worked with them in their businesses. It's conveyed to others in your actions, your behaviors, and how you made them feel. Each of those investments contributes long-term leadership equity to your legacy.

These contributions share a common trait of influencing people's actions and behaviors today and tomorrow. In that manner, they're the dividends of your investments.

Your influence doesn't stop with one action; your legacy is carried within those you impacted beyond the time you're with them. Your legacy lasts even longer as those people leave their own legacies with others. In this manner, you create a long-term leadership network by helping others improve the effectiveness of their own leadership. In the end, your leadership legacy transcends the time you spent with them.

> "Carve your name on hearts, not tombstones. A legacy is etched into the minds of others and the stories they share about you."
>
> –Shannon L. Alder

...and impact...

A legacy is formed over time and begins when you've impacted another person. While it can start at the very first meeting; more often, it's felt when you've worked with them over time, helping them, supporting them, and impacting them with your leadership. They remember you, how you enabled their success, and how they learned and developed as a result.

This remembrance brings your legacy alive. As they experience the emotions triggered by the memory, the reflections kick their learning into a higher gear. There's an emotional residue left by you that makes up your legacy. It comes from that emotional filter they apply to your actions and the behaviors that form the memory and legacy you've now left behind.

When they remember the positive legacy you left with them, they'll want to work with you again and again. More and more people begin to see you as a leader as a result of the legacy you create.

... with others...

Within the lasting nature of a leader's legacy, there's another element of legacy—it's kept in the minds and memories *of others*. As a result, *others* determine how you're remembered and perceived long-term.

When you leave a legacy, you leave it to others. Over time, leaders develop a network of people with whom they've worked. It's this network with which your legacy is left.

As you are leaving a leadership legacy, you are influencing and building your leadership network. *With others* means not just those you've developed relationships with, but also includes people you don't know directly who are in your downline and, as such, are networked to you.

What will your legacy be?

We believe that everyone leaves a legacy, intentionally or not. Leaders are mindful of their legacy, working on it every day despite the long-time horizon associated with it.

The important thing regarding mindfulness toward your legacy is to make sure that it's *your* legacy. What's important and meaningful to *you*? What are *your* core values, and how can you lead from them? Each of us has different strengths and competencies that we bring to the table. In much the same way, we each care about different things when it comes to our legacy.

Below is a collection of statements evidencing the legacies left with others. Take a moment to review those that reflect a positive legacy and those that reflect a negative legacy. They're in the third person so you can see the legacies through the eyes of others.

Positive Examples I am . . . .

- If you **really** want to know how things work, go talk to that leader.

- That leader was always reflecting and looking inward before they jumped outward.

- That leader was always present when I was with them.

- That leader inspired me to really go for my dreams.

- That leader was known for giving those who were struggling a second chance to prove themselves and restore their confidence and credibility.

- That leader broke down barriers between people.

- Working with that leader was always fun.

- That leader is remembered for their passion for the product and the business.

- That leader was respected for the way they treated people. They approached most conversations with a coach-first attitude, seeking first to understand the other person.

- That leader was known for being accountable and willing to have the team hold them accountable.

Negative Examples:

- I worked with that leader for three months, and not once did I talk with them. I just received emails and messages.

- I was having trouble, and my leader was never around because they were always too busy.

- The leader seemed friendly enough, but when I missed two team meetings due to personal problems, they didn't seem to care.

- All my leader could do was constantly tell me how to run my business.

- We had a great event, but when we all met to debrief, the only thing the leader did was talk about their leadership. I mean it sounded like they had run the whole event by themselves!

How is a legacy formed?

While people may remember a specific instance or interaction they had with you, your legacy is the sum total of all of those moments combined. It's the overall perspective people carry in their hearts and minds about you. Leaving a long-term legacy for *tomorrow* happens through your actions and interactions with people *today*.

Below are some things through which your legacy is being affected **right now**:

- Leadership Vision
- Say-do Alignment
- Role Modeling
- Leadership Engine

Leadership Vision

What's your plan for your legacy? How do you want to be remembered? Here are steps you could take to develop your legacy plan:

- **Reflect:** A focus of this book has been reflection. Take advantage of the reflection skills you've developed, and look back at other leaders who have left a legacy with you and how they made you feel.

- **Analyze and Summarize:** Take your reflections and find the themes that are important and resonate with you.

- **Write your legacy vision:** Document the long-term influence you want to have and the kind of leader you want to be.

- **Evaluate your legacy vision:** Have you aimed high enough? Is your vision realistic and achievable? Does your vision require you to grow to realize it?

- **Establish Feedback Loops**: Feedback loops help you obtain data when assessing your legacy. You may find that your ability to increase your self-awareness is positively impacted by your analysis and review of the feedback you receive. This cycle of action, self-review, feedback from others, review, and adjustment can help you monitor not only where you stand today, but also how you want to move forward.

Say/Do Alignment

In previous modules, we defined say/do gaps as the difference between saying one thing and doing another. Instead of allowing a gap to form, focus more on having say/do alignment.

How you're remembered tomorrow is partially determined by how you're seen today. It can be cemented when others see a strong alignment between what you **do** and what you **say**. Unfortunately, they also remember when you do the opposite of what you've said, which can lead to your leaving a negative legacy. Striving for say/do alignment is a foundational element of your legacy. As you consistently do what you say you'll do, you will be leaving a positive legacy of confidence, trust, and dependability.

Role Modeling

Role modeling comes from the awareness that your daily behaviors affect the legacy you want to leave. As with say/do alignment, others are watching how you walk, talk, and act. Accordingly, you have the opportunity to model the actions you value.

Some leaders feel as if they're under the magnifying glass, and, to a degree, that's correct. However, it's your *attitude* during those times when all eyes are on you that makes all the difference. Focus on the values you want to live and lead with and act with integrity. That will help you to model who you are to others.

Leadership Engine

Earlier in this book we described the Leadership Engine as comprised of credibility, relationships, trust, and influence. Our view is that establishing credibility, developing relationships, earning trust, and using influence are a part of the daily routine leaders engage in to build their leadership equity.

As leaders use the Leadership Engine with their team, they're creating their distributed *leadership network*. For advanced and skilled leaders, this leadership network can function as a way to maximize the leverage, reach, and impact of a single individual. As leaders invest in their network, they're creating leadership equity.

Leadership equity is the capital, goodwill, and currency that are generated by leaders as they go about their days. In many ways, the amount of investment (and subsequent equity) that's made by a leader ends up being their leadership legacy, and it can pay dividends for a long time. And… leadership equity is the investment into your leadership legacy.

Why focus on your legacy today?

Why do we encourage a sense of urgency about your legacy? It's because legacies are built over time, day by day. If you're not intentionally building a *positive* legacy, you run the risk of building a neutral or negative one.

While others are the ultimate judges of your legacy, you can still influence it. Ask yourself what your legacy is right now. Is it what you want it to be? How do you want to be remembered? Why is that important to you? The answers help to form the basis of your actions and behaviors today.

At the foundation of your leadership legacy is who you are as a leader. It's not "doing" leadership, it's figuring out who you are and who you want to be as a leader and *then* doing it. If leaving a lasting and positive legacy for the future is important to you, then think about who you are as a leader today and how your current actions are affecting the type of legacy you want to leave.

Here are some other reasons to focus on this today.

Investing into others creates leadership equity for the future

Just as saving a little bit of money every single day allows for compounding interest to accumulate over time, making an investment in your leadership network on a consistent basis creates a massive amount of lasting leadership equity.

> *"Legacy is not leaving something for people, it's leaving something in people."*
>
> –Peter Strople

Some of that investment may return to you directly as people work with you in the future. In other instances, the return may be felt by other people who have the benefit of working with those with whom you've left a leadership legacy.

When you invest your time, energy, and leadership in others, there will be a return that could far outpace your original investment.

As your legacy increases so does your credibility

As you leave a positive leadership legacy with others, your influence expands throughout your downline. This influence becomes part of your credibility that goes with you to the next person who joins your team. This positive influence helps you to establish credibility quickly and potentially at a deeper level with the new team members and customers. You now have a credibility foundation to build upon. The Leadership Engine keeps on working.

Difference between Legacy and Reputation

"Legacy" and "Reputation" are interrelated, but mean different things. A reputation is the beliefs or opinions that are generally held about someone or something. Your reputation can come from rumors or other nonfactual viewpoints. It usually is temporary or fleeting. Your reputation tends to be discussed in the present tense and is frequently tenuous.

Your legacy, on the other hand, is what you leave behind. It tends to be based more in actual experience. Your legacy looks at your results or actions and is a reflection of your impact. Your legacy usually represents a body of work and is long lasting.

It makes you that "go-to" leader for the team

People ask for you when the legacy you've left has been well received and they want to replicate what you did in your business. Each action you take can be used to create a positive legacy that will propel you to the front of everyone's mind when they're in need of a "go-to" leader.

Your legacy helps teammates become a part of your leadership network

You, as well as the members of your team, can use your leadership equity as a shared resource. You can call upon the network you've built in order to enable faster solutions and answers to challenges similar to those encountered earlier in your shared experiences.

One of the components of the leader's role is the large number of people with whom you have important interactions. These people become a part of your network as you invest in them. When they see and experience how you lead, influence, and achieve success, your legacy grows and your network becomes stronger. Each time you use your network, it can help to reinforce the network connections between you.

Helping others achieve success increases the impact of your leadership legacy

People will remember the successes they had with your leadership. They'll remember the events that went flawlessly and the times they achieved the next rank due in part to the help and support you provided, and they will tend to remember them as part of a positive legacy.

There are so many benefits to focusing on your legacy today! Let's move on to ways your legacy can last even longer.

How a legacy can live forever

Legacy evokes an emotional response that can last a lifetime. This is why focusing on our leadership legacy is crucial if we want to leave a positive one. The driving emotional force behind a leadership legacy is how a person felt about the leader and what their lasting response is to how the leader acted and behaved. Even more powerful is the fact that the influence of the leader can continue to be felt in other people and other businesses even though they may have never met or worked with the originating source!

> "Put simply, we found that looking forward, people wanted to achieve success in organizational or performance terms. But looking back, they wanted to know that their efforts were seen, and felt, in a positive way by the individuals they worked with directly and indirectly."
>
> –Robert Galford & Regina Maruca
>
> *Your Leadership Legacy, pg xi, 2006, Harvard Business Publishing, Boston MA*

A leadership legacy can also live on with significance through the development of another leader. This practice involves working with a person to help him or her grow his or her own leadership capabilities. The true measure of a leader is the quality of the other leaders they develop. Building up leaders is an intentional and purpose-filled journey brimming with investment after investment poured into other potential leaders.

To leave this type of legacy, the leaders you work with must have a desire to develop their own leadership skills and want to work with you as a part of it. The opportunity to do this type of work can be quite fulfilling for you and it will strengthen your legacy. You will have the chance to affect multiple generations of people through this new leader. When this happens, your influence not only extends to the person you developed, but it also extends to the people they develop and so on. In this context, your leadership legacy can be passed on generationally to many other people.

It follows that one of the measures of a leader is the leaders they leave behind. In a sense, these leaders become the legacy themselves. In athletic coaching circles, you'll hear the concept of a "coaching tree." This is formed when a coach has assistant coaches who go on to become head coaches themselves, with the pattern repeating itself until the first head coach becomes the head of a very large tree of coaches. The other coaches become the legacy of the first coach.

What if the Legacy I'm leaving is not the one I want?

Back to the real world for a moment... What if I've made mistakes, had say/do gaps, been inconsistent, unreliable, etc.? What do I do?

First, refocus on the legacy you want to leave. Make sure that legacy is clear and means something to you. Then reflect on the gaps that exist between your current actions and words and the legacy you want to leave. What changes do you need to introduce right away? Who do you need to apologize to? Where do you need to clear up any ambiguity around your goals and values?

Take a good, hard look at yourself in the mirror and get ready to do the hard work of reconciling with members of your team. There may be some crucial conversations in your future—OK, own up to that. If you truly want to leave a legacy that is different from the one you are currently leaving, then changes will have to be made.

For example, your legacy describes the kind of impact you want to have with your children. Suppose that, unfortunately, you have gotten out of balance and your business has taken higher priority too many times. Go ahead and set boundaries on your time and accessibility. Make your family, and their interests, your highest priority. Make the necessary changes in your business actions, and set new, clear expectations with your team. Even if you do reach balance, realize that nothing lasts forever, so be on the watch for when you will need to be agile again.

What is so powerful about this recalibration is that, by being humble, acknowledging where you have missed on the important things, and making changes to your behavior, you can actually reconnect with your legacy. You can actually begin to build a stronger legacy than you had thought possible! You can see the positive impact you are having and how your legacy is coming back to life within the lives of others. It doesn't get any better!

Integration and Last Review

Below is a recap of all ten modules in the Downline Leadership program and their tie-in to leaving a leadership legacy.

Module	Definition	Integration with Leadership Legacy
Downline Leadership	*The act of connecting, engaging, and influencing your team toward success.*	Becoming a leader is a conscious decision that requires a level of self-awareness, continuous growth, and learning. In much the same way, your leadership legacy is determined by your choices and how you conduct yourself day in and day out.
Leadership Engine	*Establishing credibility, developing relationships, earning trust, and gaining influence with your team and downline.*	The extent to which you've helped others achieve success and become the "go-to" leader helps you kick-start your credibility. In many situations, your legacy as a leader lives longest in the minds of the people with whom you've had a strong relationship. A leader's integrity and character are primary elements in his or her ability to build trust. This same integrity and character is frequently an integral part of creating a leadership legacy. Leaders use the influence they've gained to motivate, encourage, and lead the team. This effective use of influence leaves a legacy of leadership with people. As you model influence, people have the opportunity to use that legacy to help them to increase their own influence with others.

Module	Definition	Integration with Leadership Legacy
Communication	*Listening, caring, sharing, and connecting with your team and downline.*	Truly connecting with others leaves a special legacy. Money comes and goes, but when people know that you really care for them, your legacy is created.
Coaching	*Being a catalyst for the growth and development of others.*	Fundamentally, coaches are interested in developing and growing the people around them. This investment in a network of other leaders often becomes a legacy in and of itself.
Ownership & Accountability	*When you lay claim to something as being completely yours and accept the responsibility that drives leaders and teams toward success.*	Leaders are owners. Your legacy will reflect your being seen as an owner and how you helped your team become co-owners with you. Leaders are strongly aligned with accountability, and your legacy would be incomplete without the ability to create an accountability culture.
Intuition	*The ability to combine the hard physical data with the soft emotional data and make a decision to move forward.*	Using your intuition to reach people where they're at builds your legacy. Legacies are born and strengthened each time you listen to understand others and use your intuition for that open-ended question that penetrates their hearts.
Overcoming Challenges	*Removing the obstacles, ambiguity, and issues that hinder progress.*	All businesses have challenges. What's remembered is **how** you effectively lead the team to help them overcome their challenges, and that becomes part of your legacy.
Innovation	*The ability to think of creative ideas and put them into action.*	You have innovation as a part of your legacy when you're remembered for having inspired creativity and the implementation of ideas.
Balance and Agility	*Finding stability by being flexible and responsive to the needs of the business.*	Leaders smoothly handle leadership dichotomies and find the right balance. Achieving balance leaves a legacy that your teammates then take to their teams.
Leadership Legacy	*The lasting contribution and impact you leave with others.*	The last chapter for leaders is their legacy. What legacy are you leaving?

The Beginning of a Legacy

Two years ago... Mary remembered the night like it was just yesterday. She was hosting her first 101 class and June had come to hear about essential oils. June was like almost everyone there, interested in the oils and very engaged with Mary as she spoke, but, there was something different about June. After the class was over and Mary was breathing a sigh of relief, June came up to her.

June: Mary, were you nervous?

Mary: Man, was I ever! But, how did you know?

June: I could just tell. Your love of the oils came through big time, but you seemed pretty nervous explaining how some of the oils worked, and, when there were technical questions from the audience, you looked like you started to sweat a little.

Mary: You're so right! I didn't even realize it. You mentioned the technical elements of the oils. Is that something you're interested in?

June: Actually, I'm a chemist down the street at the lab, and yes, I'm quite interested in how the oils work.

Mary smiled to herself. I can't believe I remember that story so clearly, but why not? My life changed that night. You see June really had wanted to learn about the oils, so I found every science book I could on essential oils and gave them to June. June seemed to eat them for breakfast and was soon an expert on the oils—where they came from, why they worked, the chemical families they belonged to, why they worked better in some combinations than in others, and how to apply them for maximum benefit. June and I ended up working the business together, and now our 101 class has two sides to it—the passion side and the science side. Our business is doing extremely well as many millennials want to know the science stuff (so many nerds out there) and don't settle for what I alone would have shared with them. Our customers are so much better informed from June's research that they're using many more of the oils and in a lot more circumstances.

It's funny how having someone see something in you, and you seeing something in them, can be such a game changer. Yep, that was the beginning of a legacy for both of us!

Discussion

Both June and Mary chose to invest into each other. Even the most unlikely of pairings can produce a rich legacy.

As you contemplate your journey, your evolution as a leader, and your legacy, consider that the best time to start your legacy might be right now.

The Path Forward

At the beginning of this book we asked two questions; take a moment to answer them:

- Do you see yourself as a leader?
- Do others see you as a leader?

Those were the questions that started us on this journey. The questions to ask yourself now, as we near the end of this program, are

- What type of legacy are you leaving?

- Why is it important to you?

- Why do you need to manage it daily?

- How do you want to be remembered?

- How does your legacy impact others?

- What other leaders have you developed?

As you reflect upon this module, consider what you're doing each day to leave **your** leadership legacy.

Final Word On Downline Leadership

You've been through ten modules honing your Downline Leadership. Time to reflect on where we began:

How is it possible that a downline that is well managed fails to achieve its goals? Frequently, it is due to a lack of leadership. The team needs someone to rally them when things are stalled, guide them when the vision gets murky, and coach them when they are stuck. They need someone to influence them in a new direction, celebrate when a milestone is reached, or hold them accountable to goals they have set for themselves. They need a leader!

That leader is you! Take what you've learned and put it into practice. Help your team to become owners and leaders who make a difference. YOU CAN DO IT!

Action Required

Please complete the exercise on the next page.

Discussion Framework:

Use this page to capture your preliminary thoughts about this module's content. Each quadrant has questions that are provided to help stimulate your thoughts and reflections. This is not a quiz and there are no wrong answers. It's an opportunity to deepen self-awareness, so capture whatever seems appropriate to you.

	INTERNAL	EXTERNAL
INDIVIDUAL	**REFLECT** What did you read about this week that caught your eye and caused you to reflect? p18 break down of 177 - Re address	**ADOPT** What would you like to adopt as a going-forward behavior or process that you picked up from this week's module? Say do adopt. p177-178
GROUP	**INQUIRE** What question would you like to ask the group concerning the topic(s) in the module? p180	**SHARE** What insight, principle, or leadership precept did you want to share with the group?

ERIC WALTON

As President of Building Up Leaders LLC, Eric Walton has been coaching leaders around the world from diverse industries such as direct selling (multi-level marketing), high tech, manufacturing, banking, and others.

Mr. Walton is a founding partner of the John Maxwell Team and a certified leadership coach, trainer, and speaker. Mr. Walton has written and developed three different leadership programs: **Downline Leadership**, **Project Leadership**, and **Process Leadership**. He has been working alongside his wife, Tammy Walton, for the past four years as she has achieved the Diamond rank as a distributor of essential oils for Young Living.

Prior to founding Building Up Leaders, Eric Walton spent more than thirty years as an accomplished leader and executive in the high-tech industry. During that time he was focused on raising leaders and was directly involved in the advancement of hundreds of managers, directors, and vice-presidents, while training and coaching many more. During his rich leadership experience he held several COO positions at influential mid-size tech firms, as well as being an executive at Fortune 500 firms. Eric's leadership and management experience in multiple functional areas has afforded him a broad experience and insight into technology, finance, marketing, sales, and operations and has included management responsibility for more than 2000 people.

It is this experience that has proven invaluable in understanding leadership issues across a multitude of markets, industries, and locations, managing teams to solve those problems, and raising up leaders to get it done.

Mr. Walton received a BS in Business Management from University at Albany and a MBA from the University of Arizona.

TIME TO LEAD!

Building Up Leaders wants to join you on your leadership journey. We will inspire you, encourage you, challenge you, and develop you. Here's how we can help you:

- **Coaching** – The best way to engage with the leadership material in this book is in a small group lead by a coach. Join one of our small groups to go through the Downline Leadership program and change your leadership skills forever.

- **Resources** – Find the tools you need to raise your leadership and that of your team.

- **Events/Speaking** – Come see us at our next live event to experience leadership in action! Better yet, contact us about speaking at your next event!

For more information go to www.BuildingUpLeaders.com.

☐ 3 Bundles + drawing for oil shelf.

☐ Seedlings
☐ Pet Bundle
☐ ~~Dead thitcles Bu~~ Spa Bundle

Last day 31st